JonBenet Knows Evil Love

JonBenet Knows Evil Love

Richard Rubacher

Writers Club Press
San Jose New York Lincoln Shanghai

JonBenet Knows Evil Love

All Rights Reserved © 2000 by Richard Rubacher

No part of this book may be reproduced or transmitted in any form or by any means, graphic, electronic, or mechanical, including photocopying, recording, taping, or by any information storage or retrieval system, without the permission in writing from the publisher.

Published by Writers Club Press
an imprint of iUniverse.com, Inc.

For information address:
iUniverse.com, Inc.
620 North 48th Street
Suite 201
Lincoln, NE 68504-3467
www.iuniverse.com

ISBN: 0-595-09040-0

Printed in the United States of America

Dedication

To Gail Wilts, my research partner and co-host of our former radio show. You found JonBenet's cry for help that was hidden in her song. Your penetration into her psyche led to the title of this book.

To David Oates, the founder and developer of Reverse Speech technology. You made sense out of what most of us thought was nonsense. You understood the mysterious references to our inner voice mentioned by Shakespeare, T.S. Eliot and the Bible. I agree with Larry Dossey's statement that your discovery "is of Nobel Prize caliber."

Contents

Dedication v

A Personal Note to Jon and Patsy Ramsey ix

Acknowledgements xi

Visit Our Website xiii

What the Bible, Shakespeare
    and T.S. Eliot Have in Common xv

What Is Reverse Speech
    and Embedded Communication? xvii

Introduction xxi

Chapter One: The New Technology,
              a Confessional Box 1

Chapter Two: How O.J. Simpson
              "Did in" Judge Ito 5

Chapter Three: The Ramseys' First
               Fatal Flaw 11

Chapter Four: Highlights of the Technology
              on Our Radio Program 31

Chapter Five: The Ramseys Second Fatal Flaw
—They Talk Again 49

Chapter Six: The Bible, Shakespeare, T.S. Eliot
& Know It 61

Chapter Seven: Different Ways the Ramseys Bury
Themselves—a Cross Reference
Guide (AKA the Smoking Guns) 65

Chapter Eight: Closing Arguments 83

Afterword 97

Appendix 99

A Personal Note to Jon and Patsy Ramsey

My associate* and I wish to meet with you privately so we can go over the abundance of information the two of you have revealed through the verbal messages that came from your two CNN press conferences in 1997. You also appeared in the ninety minute British documentary that was cablecast in the United States in October 1998. We would like you to hear your forward and backward statements. First we will play some of the statements you made in your forward voice. This is the voice of your conscious mind or ego. Then we will replay the remarks in reverse. This is the voice of your unconscious.

You will note the discrepancy between the comments made by the conscious and unconscious. This experience will benefit you in terms of personal, physical and psychological growth.

We look forward to breaking bread with you. Please see our detailed note in Chapter Eight, "Closing Arguments—Jon and Patsy's Trial in the Spiritual Court." The Voice behind your voice— "the still small voice" — keeps sending you 911 calls through your dreams, nightmares and haunting memories.

---

* Gail Wilts, my associate and co-host of our former weekly radio program in San Francisco, is the person who decoded JonBenet's "I know evil love" message.

Acknowledgements

Eternal gratitude is expressed to Gail Wilts, who I met at the first Reverse Speech convention that was held in Los Angeles in January 1997. Gail spent hours going over the various renditions of JonBenet singing "I want to be a cowboy singer." When she located **Mommy, now I know evil love** (Note: following protocol, all Reversals or Embedded Communications are given in **bold type**) Gail sent me the sound file through email. I transferred the forward statement onto the Reverse Speech machine to confirm her finding. Then I asked Elyce Curtis, a San Francisco Bay Area psychic, to listen to the playback. She agreed with Gail's analysis. Elyce's twenty-two year old son, Traegen, a man with a trained ear, was asked to listen to the recording in reverse. In order not to influence his judgment, he was not told about the contents of the message.

Mommy, now I know evil love—"is what I hear," Traegen said. This was wonderful. We didn't tell him that there were actually six words in JonBenet's message. Nor did we tell him that the last word was interrupted or cut off or drowned out by the music.

Gail and I spent days analyzing the two CCN interviews given by the Ramseys. We spent a week together foraging through the October 1998 documentary that was cablecast on the Arts & Entertainment Network (A&E).

Gratitude also goes to the producer and interviewer of the October 1998 Ramseys documentary that was created in England and broadcast in Great Britain and cablecast in the United States through A&E.

As you may know, the English producer's goal was to tell the Ramsey side of the story. Instead of attacking and/or accusing the Ramseys of complicity in JonBenet's murder, the interviewer befriended the parents. No hostile questions were given. A cordial, respectful, even reverential tone, characterized the session in this ninety-minute documentary. The result was tailor made for reversals of a colossal magnitude. By being on their side, Jon and Patsy Ramsey felt secure. This made them relaxed. The results astounded Gail and myself. Not only did the Ramseys open up—through their reversals—even their sister, Pam Paugh and the Ramseys attorney, Bryan Morgan, fell prey to the loving style of the interviewer.

Not only did Jon and Patsy Ramsey provide additional information about their role in JonBenet's murder, the sister and attorney also revealed their complicity in the crime.

Gratitude is given to my New York literary agent, Jeff Herman—who placed the commercially and spiritually successful *Chicken Soup For The Soul* series. Jeff was unable to find a publisher for *JonBenet Knows Evil Love*. No one wanted to take a risk with this new technology. Jeff Herman was the first *influential* person in the literary world who believed in the new technology that eavesdrops on the psyche.

Final gratitude is expressed to my life-long friend, Elizabeth Allred of Sacramento, California. She saved my life during my hunger strike against the legislative body of California several years ago.

Visit Our Website

www.EvilLoveJonBenet.com

Another site of interest is www.ReverseSpeech.com. This is the site of David Oates, the founder of Reverse Speech.

The JonBenet website provides the reader with the opportunity to HEAR the actual words of JonBenet and her parents. You will HEAR the forward statement, which is the conscious mind speaking. Then you will HEAR the words spoken in reverse. These words are from the unconscious or psyche.

Included in the site is the list of prominent people who believe in their heart that Jon and Patsy Ramsey are involved in the murder of their daughter.

Information about the other works of the author is found.

Periodic updates are given.

What the Bible, Shakespeare and T.S. Eliot Have in Common

"Your own lips bear witness against you" (Job 15:6 King James Version). The bard penned these words in The Tempest, Act II, Scene II (A.D. 1611).

> *His forward voice, now is to*
> speak well of his friend; His
> backward voice is to utter
> foul speeches and to detract.

In today's language, the "forward voice" is known by many names. The conscious mind, ego and the "persona"—that is, the self that we present to the public.

The "backward voice" is also known by a variety of names. The unconscious, the psyche, the spiritual self, the wisdom part of us, the holy ghost, the indwelling spirit and "the still small voice" that is reported in the Old Testament. The New Testament (the gospel of John) mentions the paradox where "the word was made flesh."

"The word behind the word" (T.S. Eliot, *Gerontion*, 1920).

What Is Reverse Speech and Embedded Communication?

In several email messages to my friend Paula Doughty questions about the technology that eavesdrops on the human psyche were exchanged. Here are the results of the exchange.

When we speak, two messages are given simultaneously. One message is delivered in our forward voice. The other message is contained in our backward voice. The forward voice is the conscious mind speaking. The backward voice is the unconscious speaking. In other words, the brain is able to transmit verbal messages on two tracks simultaneously. Hidden messages are found not only when we speak words. The brain has the capacity to make intelligible words from a grunt. A woman had trouble with her young son who was afflicted with cerebral palsy. Most of the time she was unable to decipher her son's speech. He became frustrated and began to act out violently in school. When she heard that Reverse Speech is able to decipher messages from grunts, she went to a Reverse Speech analyst. She heard her son speaking on playback. His psyche said, **where is your love, mom?** The boy also heard the playback. This was the first time he heard himself communicate in a manner that was understood.

Even laughter can contain a cryptic clearly heard message from the psyche. When we cough during a conversation, a playback on the Reverse Machine enables us to hear a word or phrase spoken by the psyche. We literally "cough up" hidden material from the depths of our being. A sigh, when analyzed, can result in a reversal.

When we speak the truth, the message from the conscious and unconscious are in harmony. This is known as a congruent message.

When we lie, the message from the unconscious differs from the forward statement. The new technology enables us to eavesdrop on the unconscious, we actually HEAR, in our own voice, what our unconscious says. When a lie is caught by the unconscious, the statement is inharmonious or incongruent.

This is both wonderful and dreadful.

Even Freudian slips are picked up in the reversals. Jon Ramsey made this Freudian slip, **I went downSCARES.** In his forward voice he said, "I went downstairs." The statement was made when the police were in the house on the day that JonBenet's body was discovered. He was worried if his and Patsy's story would be credible to the woman detective who was in the house when the body was discovered. Patsy made a statement about JonBenet. When played on the Reversing Machine, we found this revealing remark, **you lady mannequin.** This shows the mom's attitude toward JonBenet. As we know, a **mannequin** has no feelings. It is treated like an object.

Jon Ramsey made a statement that many Americans offered him sympathy through letters. He talked about a little girl who corresponds with him. His reversal contains four sexual innuendoes. **Nice little girl. Let me look. Let me nurse you. You get down on my fire.**

The messages from the psyche are heard one of two ways, Paula. Through the Reversing Machine that I mentioned before. It's a tape recorder that has the ability to play back in a very slow speed what was spoken in the forward voice. The message can also be played back on the computer thru Real Player. The disadvantage of Real Player is that you cannot slow the player down to the slow play that is found on the Reversing Machine.

"Once more, for clarification," Paula wrote. "Do you take a recording of a statement and then play it backwards to get the reverse message?"

That's right. It's played back on the Reverse Speech machine or thru Real Player on your computer.

Sometimes additional information accompanies the untruth, providing insights about the secret motivation and hidden agenda of the speaker.

It's a show you're running, Jon Ramsey said in a reversal. In his forward statement he said that he is holding the press conference to announce that he hired a special investigative team to catch the killer or killers of his daughter. By eavesdropping on his psyche, we learned about his secret motive and "hidden agenda." He is using the press conference to deceive the media and the American public by putting on **a show.**

The difference between the lie detector (examining physiological responses) and Reverse Speech (examining verbal speech and verbal responses—laughter, coughing, sighing) are discussed in Chapter Four, "Highlights of our weekly radio show—the psyche does not lie," and Chapter Eight, "Closing Arguments."

Several experiments were conducted on our weekly radio program from skeptics who wanted to disprove Reverse Speech. See Chapter Four, "Highlights of our weekly radio show" for a report on the skeptics and the experiments to deliberately lie to the Reverse Speech machine.

Introduction

Introduction: JonBenet, the whistle blower.

In American slang, "to sing" means blowing the whistle on someone. Through an ironic twist, JonBenet Ramsey sings a song that continues to haunt her parents. The hidden message in the child's forward words opens the floodgates on the sexual crime committed by her father.

A video clip of JonBenet Ramsey shows her dressed in a Western outfit. In the clip, she sings one line, "I want to be a cowboy singer."

When played on the Reverse Speech machine, her words are, **Mommy, now I know evil love.**

Note: All the reversals are displayed in **bold face type** to distinguish them from the speaker's forward comments. Listen many times. It takes a while to get used to hearing words when they are spoken backwards. At first it may sound like gibberish and nonsensical noise. Then the "aha moment" comes as you clearly distinguish words, the voice behind the voice, the voice of the psyche. Listen to the seven words sung by JonBenet, **Mommy, now I know evil love.** The first six words are clear and precise. The final word, **love**, is fragmented. You will hear **love**— Some people, including Gail Wilts, claim they also hear JonBenet pronounce the entire word **love**, in a clear voice.

As will be seen in Chapter Two, "This Technology Blesses O.J.Simpson," a reversal makes known the speaker's true thoughts, feelings and emotions. A reversal is found when the tape-recorded statement is played backwards on the Reversing Machine, a technological breakthrough that resulted in the name of David Oates to be placed before the selection committee of the Nobel Prize. David Oates is the founder and developer of this technology.

When you tune into our Website you will hear JonBenet singing, "I want to be a cowboy singer."

On the Website you will then hear the reversal, where she says, **Mommy, now I know evil love.**

More on the parents knowledge of the child's seduction is in Chapter Three, "The Ramseys' First Fatal Flaw."

Evil love is an expression of JonBenet's grief over her parents' betrayal.

Yet another level of meaning, which is speculative on our part, is that the parents panicked when their unconscious mind tuned into the veiled threat contained in the child's reversal. **Mommy, now I know evil love** indicates JonBenet was of the age where she knew the sex stuff was wrong and intended to publicize it. In Chapter One: "The New Technology is a Confessional Box," there is an unconscious communication between Judge Ito and O.J. during the jury selection process. Judge Ito and O.J. engage in a give-and-take exchange. Judge Ito says, "Mr. Simpson, do you understand that we will be continuing the date that we previously selected to start jury selection from September 19th to September 26th? Do you understand that involves extending your right to a speedy trial by seven days?"

His Honor's words from the unconscious: **Simpson killed them.**

Simpson replied to the judge's surprising revelation. In his forward voice, Simpson said, "Yes, I do your honor."

When his forward statement was played back on the Reversing Machine, Simpson's reversal said, **I did it.**

In this dialogue, Simpson's unconscious mind resonated with Judge Ito. That is, Simpson's unconscious and the Judge's unconscious communicated in the language of the psyche. It is speculated that Judge It's finding O.J. Simpson guilty may have resulted in the judge's leaning over backwards during the trial to favor the defense team. To prove that a fair trial was being conducted, the judge allowed an avalanche of irrelevant testimony, including the introduction of the "N-word" from the defense, and the haranguing of the prosecution's witnesses (remember Barry

Scheck taunting the police crime lab technician, Mr Fung), to be heard in front of the jury.

In his own mind, Judge Ito felt guilty about pronouncing the defendant guilty by delving below the tip of the iceberg and into the unconscious mind of the fallen football hero. Unconsciously, the judge could not forgive himself for violating his professional code of ethics, which declares the magistrate remains impartial during the proceedings.

Returning to **Mommy, now I know evil love.** One or both parents may have tuned into JonBenet's unconscious when she sang the cowboy song at a competitive event, *before an audience of judges.* It is conceivable that panic ensued. Might she go public to broadcast her family's betrayal? Instead of pouring out her discontent through the unconscious, she might come "straight out" and betray the ones who betrayed her. More on this in Chapter Two, "How O.J. Simpson 'did in' Judge Ito."

Chapter One

The New Technology, a Confessional Box

The time has come to bury the Ramseys so they can have a spiritual re-birth. Through the technology that eavesdrops on the psyche, we learn that Patsy Ramsey wants to end the haunting images found in her dreams and nightmares.

By reading this book Jon and Patsy Ramsey will understand the futility in trying to hide **our crime** (the words spoken by Patsy Ramsey's unconscious in the 1997 CNN televised press conference).

If the Ramseys have no knowledge about the contents of this work, someone close to them, like their attorney, Bryan Morgan or Patsy's sister Pam Paugh, or a close friend of the family can get the damaging information presented here to Jon and Patsy. This would be a truly friendly gesture. The Ramseys will be able to hear the voice of their psyche telling them what the hidden meanings are of the words that flow from them.

Through this technology that was made available in the United States by the Australian David Jon Oates, the parents have entered the "confessional box" where the dark recesses and inner chambers of their minds are exposed to public scrutiny.

Through this technology that bares the soul, also known as the psyche and unconscious mind, Jon and Patsy Ramsey open Pandora's Box, releasing the horrors of the physical, mental and psychological crimes they committed against JonBenet. The crimes include murder, incest and cold indifference toward their daughter (**you lady mannequin** are the words used by the unconscious mind of the mother to describe her demised daughter).

Jon and Patsy Ramsey confess to their involvement in killing JonBenet. In the mother's revealing reversals. **Oh I'm that person** Patsy said, referring to the "person out there" who killed her daughter. Her psyche, the part of her that does not lie, wanted no part in the cover up. It accused her by saying **Oh I'm that person.**

I done it Jon said. Neither was his psyche about to lie for him. **You're a bad person for doing it.** This indicates he feels guilty for killing his daughter. Shortly we will read about his sexual relationship with JonBenet.

And I planned the note (Patsy). **That little crime messed up** (Jon). **I know you've sinned** (Patsy). **Our crime** (Patsy).

In the traditional court of law, attorneys for both sides *probe the conscious mind*. This aspect of the mind, referred to as the tip of the iceberg, has severe limitations. Exploration of the conscious, rational mind cannot access the hidden agenda and secret motives that are buried in the unconscious. Nor will the hidden agenda and dark motives be honestly presented in a forthright manner by the defendant or other witnesses. As we know, on the witness stand in a court of criminal or civil law, people lie to protect themselves or to prevent harm from coming to someone they care about.

Through this technology the vastness of the *submerged iceberg known as the unconscious* is now opened to public scrutiny. In Chapter Eight, "Closing Arguments," we convene the Spiritual Court of Law, where the Ramseys undergo a different kind of interrogation. Our merciless exploration of the unconscious enables us to access the nightmares and scary dreams of the Ramseys. By probing into the previously inaccessible regions of the parents' psyche, we are provided with information about the recurring thoughts that haunt the Ramseys. The disturbing thoughts that suddenly appear on the screen of their conscious minds during their waking hours are also made available to us.

As stated previously, through technology, the private thoughts of the Ramseys are no longer private.

The "secret" feelings, desires and fantasies of the parents are also made public.

The parents can hide their true thoughts and feelings in a traditional court of law. Not so in the Spiritual Court of Law.

As mentioned earlier, this work is presented as a gift to Jon and Patsy. By reflecting on what their souls tell them since the murder of JonBenet, their suffering will come to an end. The father said, in a revealing reversal, **I scared.** The mother said, in another revealing moment when the psyche said, **I did it.** In the October 1998 English documentary the father's unconscious made this Freudian slip, **I walked downSCARES** (see Chapter Five: The Ramseys Third Fatal Flaw—they talk yet again).

While the conscious mind is the tip of the iceberg and makes up ten percent of the personality, we recognize that this ten-percent to be analyzed and held sacred comprises a partial aspect of a person. The hidden layers that contains the defense mechanisms and submerged depths of the entire person are not accounted for.

Some of testimony is taken from the CNN press conferences staged by the Ramseys in 1997. More evidence is obtained, (see Chapter Five "The Ramseys Second Fatal Flaw), when the parents gave the go-ahead to the British documentary that aired in the United States on the A&E Network on October 13, 1998.

Chapter Two

How O.J. Simpson "Did in" Judge Ito

O.J. Simpson is credited for launching the technology of the psyche onto the American spotlight. Through O.J.'s words, this technology came of age. The fallen hero's statement "…just turn a tape recorder on…and play it back. You will not believe that was you." David Oates, the Australian, the founder and developer of this technology, took O.J.'s advice.

As you will see and HEAR (through tuning into our Website) O.J.'s own words return to haunt him and illuminate the dramatic power of this technology. With a minimum of words produced through his speech reversals, explosive information is revealed. O.J. says that he virtually beheaded Ron Goldman; we will read that O.J. uncovers his motive for killing Nicole; we will read his story about his life long friend and football teammate, Al Cowlings (the driver of the Broncho on the Los Angeles freeway chase), was aware of the double murders. In a courtroom exchange between O.J. and Judge Ito, the magistrate declare that O.J. is guilty of killing Nicole Simpson and Ron Goldman. In the psyche-to-psyche talk, the unconscious mind of the killer and the unconscious mind of the judge are in rapport.

Such is the power of this awe-ful and aw-ful technology.

What is this technology all about? When we record and play the taped statement backwards on the technological-breakthrough device (known as the Reversing Machine), several things happen.

First, when we speak the truth in our forward voice, between the gibberish and nonsense, our backward voice will confirm that we are in the truth. In essence, there is no "betrayal."

Second, when we tell a lie in our forward voice and play the statement backwards on the Reversing Machine, there are periods of lucidity between the gibberish and nonsense. A clear word or phrase becomes distinct from the gibberish, revealing a lie.

Bless you, O.J.

Let us go to O.J. Simpson. Bless you, O.J., for talking and talking and talking. This is what O.J. said in his forward voice: "That, when she (Nicole) had some very emotional issues, with the men that she was involved with, she came to me. I don't think a woman would do that if she felt that this person was insensitive or abusive and certainly not jealous or possessive."

In his forward voice, Saint Simpson is telling us that he is a compassionate man. He parades his holy nature to us. Carl Jung called this the persona, or the mask that we wear in public. Instead of revealing our motives, the persona acts to conceal.

When played in reverse, his psyche says, **Damn your lust. Never see lovers.** (Note: following the protocol of Reverse Speech, all the messages from the psyche are displayed in **bold type**.)

O.J. spoke forty-seven words in his forward statement. Backwards, he used six words. The economical and concise part of him spoke harsh words to Nicole, **Damn your lust.** What he said in his forward voice contradicted his real feelings and thoughts about Nicole. This revealing reversal also serves as part of his confession. The next reversal indicates his fury toward Nicole: **Never see lovers.** It turned out to be a prophetic warning. O.J. took action to make sure she never saw lovers again.

In the six words contained in the reversal, O.J. has plunged the knife into himself. Unwittingly, he opened his heart.

From Saint to Sinner. This demonstrates the power and meaning that characterizes this technology. In his forward voice, he is an angel. Not so in his other Voice—the whispering of his soul or psyche.

In another instance O.J. exhibits his charm and is intent on seducing the TV host and his television viewers. His forward voice says, "I've been a good American (pause), I'm just as innocent as (pause) any of them. I should have the right to support my family and earn a living and they have been blocking me."

He's telling us the American media has thwarted or blocked him from telling his true story. This is his concealing self speaking. When his forward statement is played in reverse, we learn there is no relationship between what he is trying to say and what he truly means. We proceed from concealing to revealing when his psyche speaks: **He cowed when you missed your aim. He cowed my bayonet.**

In his mind, he is present at the crime scene on Bundy Drive (Nicole's home). O.J. is re-enacting the murder. He sees Ron Goldman elude the knife blade by ducking (**cowed**) when the first plunge was missed.

He cowed when you missed your aim. He cowed my bayonet. This revealing reversal taps into O.J.'s thoughts.

The playback on the Reversing Machine captures what is taking place in our heart. This is one of the reasons why David Oates, the founder and developer of this technology, has been placed before the nominating committee of the Nobel Award.

The interviewer says to O.J.—"White Americans believe you are guilty."

In his forward voice O.J. says, "I—I can't take that as the whole world of white Americans. Maybe there's a lot of them out there that do…"

The reversal on has nothing to do with O.J.'s forward statement. O.J. says, through the voice of his psyche, **Al was against the crime.**

The "secret" thought is expressed in clear language. This is heard when you listen to the conversation on our Website. We see there is no relationship between what he said and what he was thinking. In this revealing reversal, O.J. tells us something that was withheld from both juries in the criminal and civil trials. O.J. acknowledges, in this revealing reversal, that his life-long friend and football teammate Al Cowlings, the driver during the Bronco car chase, knew that O.J. killed Nicole and Ron Goldman. We do not know how soon after the double murders that O.J. confessed to his friend. This incredible irony is what helped to launch this technology onto the American stage.

O.J. says this through his conscious mind. "Well, the worst thing you can have—that you can ever have—is have your argument taped. I would say anybody out there that is married or in a relationship, just turn a tape recorder on the next time you have an argument and play it back. You will not believe that was you."

"…just turn a tape recorder on the next time you have an argument and play it back. You will not believe that was you."

Okay, O.J., we will follow your advice and play the tape back to hear what you said in your unconscious voice. **I skinned them all.**

"Skinned" in black slang means to con or to fool. It's curious that "skinned" also means to kill, as in skinning Nicole and Ron.

Judge Ito's secret motive for kowtowing to the defense team

Here is the scenario. During one of the pre-trial arraignment hearings, Judge Ito and O.J. engaged in a give-and-take exchange. Judge Ito said (once again, this can be heard on our Website) "Mr. Simpson, do you understand that we will be continuing the date that we previously selected to start jury selection from September 19th to September 26th? Do you understand that involves extending your right to a speedy trial by seven days?"

His Honor's words as delivered from his unconscious: **Simpson killed them.**

Simpson's immediate reply in his conscious voice. "Yes, I do your honor."

Simpson's unconscious said this, **I did it.**

In this dialogue, Simpson's unconscious mind resonated with Judge Ito. That is, Simpson's unconscious and the Judge's unconscious are communicating in the language of the psyche. It is speculated that Judge Ito's finding O.J. Simpson guilty so early in the case may have resulted in the judge's subsequent leaning over backwards during the trial to favor the DreamTeam. To prove that a fair trial was being conducted, the judge allowed an avalanche of irrelevant testimony, including the introduction of the "N-word" from the defense, to be heard in front of the jury.

Before closing out the O.J. section, it is worthwhile to provide *two examples* that show O.J. suffers guilt feelings over the murders. In his forward statements, he does not acknowledge that his daydreams, night dreams and nightmares torment him. Here is one of numerous statements that indicate O.J.'s soul has convicted him.

Forward, O.J. says, "That was my first attempt, NBC and I would have spoken on NBC, but I had for the first time…new lawyers, Bob Baker and Phil Baker, they felt that they would prefer to have time with me."

His telegraphic and cryptic reversal: **I fear the dead wife.**

Notice the present tense. **I fear.** This is the true reason why he declined to appear on NBC after the civil trial found him liable for the death of Nicole.

Forward, O.J. says, "I hope that I get a chance to sit down with you after the video is out and then we'll talk about that party. When you've seen the video I'll come back on your show and we'll talk about that alleged party."

His revealing reversal. **Still I live with the fact. I live with this in you.**

Once again, the comment is expressed in the present tense. The killing continues to haunt O.J. Until there is resolution, his conscious mind will continue to flash images of his crime. Perhaps he will make a public confession. If he does not, he is doomed, much like Raskolnikov in Doestoevsky's novel, *Crime and Punishment.*

Chapter Three

The Ramseys' First Fatal Flaw

Jon and Patsy Ramsey ignored the sage advice given by their attorneys that "silence is golden." The Ramseys, bless their souls, decided to hold the press conference that was televised by the CNN Network to its worldwide audience in 1997.

By taking center stage and having the spotlight on them, we are able to discover Jon and Patsy Ramsey's "word behind the word" (T.S. Eliot).

We are able to tune into the Ramseys' "backward voice" and decode the "foul speeches" that Shakespeare was aware of in the 17th century when he described the awesome power of the human mind. The bard intuitively grasped that we speak in the forward voice (the conscious mind) and the backward voice (the unconscious or psyche).

We realize the biblical insights have application to modern society. "He will turn their own tongue against them and bring them to ruin." (Psalms 64:8). "Your own mouth condemns you" (Job 15:6).

By taking center stage and having the spotlight on them at the CNN press conferences, the content of Jon and Patsy's unconscious became conscious.

The CNN press conferences as a confessional box

Patsy, in her forward voice says. "We feel that there are at least two people on the face of the earth that know who did this and that is the killer and someone else that person may have confided in."

Patsy, in her backward voice, **Oh I'm that person. Safe and I'll beat this. Seen that rape.**

David Oates, the founder and developer of this technology, credits Tony Feo of Harrisburg, North Carolina, for decoding the hidden meaning of Patsy Ramsey's forward words. Oates asks the question, "Is this the smoking gun in the Ramsey case?"

This and what follows provide an answer in the affirmative. As we proceed with the journey into the psyche of the Ramseys, we will uncover an outpouring of smoking guns.

Oh I'm that person. This is Patsy's opening statement. Her unconscious refuses to waste time in petty talk. It wants her to use the confessional box to announce in her forward voice what has taken place. But Patsy has free choice to accept or decline her soul's cry to tell the truth. She is not ready. But we are in a position to make her unconscious mind conscious, which is the heart and soul of this technology.

The second reversal that was uncovered in Patsy's opening statement, **Safe and I'll beat this.** In this early stage of the televised press conference Patsy expresses confidence that assembling the media is a good idea. She and her husband have nothing to worry about. The story they rehearsed will woo the media. They will obtain sympathy from the public.

The third reversal in her opening statement, **Seen that rape.** Patsy is focusing on the disturbing thought that, as we shall see during the progression of the press conference, refuses to go away.

Jon Ramsey takes the microphone. Forward, he says, "at least up until yesterday anytime spent looking at us is time wasted and that in part is why we brought in an investigative team as well to immediately look in other directions."

The smoking gun

His opening statement contains two reversals. **Oh I done it. It's a show you're running.**

On one level, his reversal indicates he spoke a lie in his forward statement.

Like his wife's opening statement, Jon's psyche wastes no time in getting to the heart of the matter. **Oh I done it.** His psyche wants him to turn the press conference into a public confession. Like his wife, he too has free choice to ignore the prompting of his soul. **Oh I done it** also lets the world know about his participation in the murder of his daughter. Another smoking gun.

The "shadow" (named by Carl Jung) part of the psyche, now surfaces. The shadow contains our dark side. When the ego is tamed, the darkness dissolves into light. **It's a show you're running,** the shadow says, serving to perpetuate the lie. But even this lie serves as a confession as Jon Ramsey admits that the real reason for hiring the investigative team was to deceive the media and American public by putting on **a show.** This reversal is in harmony with his wife's opening statement where we are informed that their "act" was orchestrated.

In his forward voice Jon says, "…to those of you who may want to ask let me address very directly. I did not kill my daughter, JonBenet."

By eavesdropping into his psyche, *four damaging reversal surface.* **And the mikes are all dumb. Voice found it out. Serve evil. Now we hate.**

We speculate that **mikes** is short for microphones and refers to the media as being the **dumb** ones, since he appears to be having his way with them. The press representatives are patiently playing by the ground rules that have been laid down. Jon and Patsy are to make statements. They are not to be confronted him with challenging questions.

The next reversal tantalizes us. While Jon Ramsey is confident about orchestrating the media, his unconscious is beginning to torment him. Doubt now engulfs him. **Voice found it out** indicates his realization that breaking the silence may have catastrophic results for him and Patsy.

Like a nightmare or scary dream, this technology is dreadful and wonderful. When we fail to "get" the message the nightmare is giving us, there is dread and panic. When we do "get" the message, the nightmare or scary dream becomes a wonderful friend. For example, falling in a lake and drowning is dreadful. The lake is a symbol for the emotional difficulty we refuse to face. By ignoring the problem, we are in effect drowning. By having the courage to face the difficulty, we will find the emotional strength to sail the troubled waters into a safe harbor.

The third reversal, **Serve evil**. His deception and deviousness are not truly helping him but are serving evil. This is another suggestion from the spiritual side of Jon Ramsey to be truthful.

The fourth reversal, **Now we hate**. This indicates he is not ready to bare his soul.

In another segment of the press conference, Jon says in his forward voice, "There have been innuendoes that she has been or was sexually molested. I can tell you they were the most hurtful innuendoes to us as a family."

Through eavesdropping his statement reads, **know for the next time but they're so ugly yes.**

If there is a **next time** he **knows** he must continue to be clever to avoid detection in the future of his illegal sexual activity. The innuendoes hurt **and they're so ugly yes** .

His conscious and unconscious are in harmony about his pain.

Patsy says, "I'm Patsy Ramsey, JonBenet's mother…"

The reversal, **And I planned the note.**

While she was saying her name in her forward voice, her thought was about the ransom note she planned. This is another confession, another smoking gun.

Patsy continues, "…but let me assure you that I did not kill JonBenet. I did not have anything to do with it…"

Smoking guns galore

By traveling below the tip of the iceberg (the conscious mind) Patsy reveals two reversals, **Your shame. You feel it.**

This is smoking gun number five as she confesses and finds it difficult to deal with the **shame**.

Patsy continues, "We made a firm commitment that we would not speak openly until we had spent time interviewing with the authorities."

Below the iceberg, **See your faith.**

Patsy's soul speaks to her in a soft whisper, reminding her, in a non-accusatory manner, that she continues to focus on the tip of the iceberg—her conscious mind. **See your faith** is another way of saying, "when you are ready, check into headquarters, the spiritual part of you, where your God-nature resides. Teresa of Avila called this aspect of us "the interior castle." Christ reminded his followers that faith makes its home within the flesh. When Patsy is ready to listen to the prompting of her soul, she will open her heart to the flame that is currently a spark but waits patiently to be stoked into a roaring fire.

In her forward voice Patsy used twenty words to communicate a lie and continue the deception. In her reversal three words were spoken. **See your faith.** In its compact, cryptic and telegraphic manner, the unconscious once again proves Jerry Brown's dictum he pronounced when he was the governor of California—"less is more."

Patsy forward, "…quite frankly over the past months it has not been real easy to talk with anyone…" She cries as she talks. The tears express her inner conflict, as will become evident by eavesdropping on her psyche. **I'm still a snob. I don't mean it.**

These revealing reversals enable us to journey into the depths of Patsy Ramsey's psyche. With these two simple statements, she bares her soul. We see Patsy in her naked, unconcealed self. Her persona and public image try to conceal but her still small voice reveals.

Being a **snob** has no rewards, no satisfactions in terms of creating a human relationship where she can confide in someone outside the immediate family. Patsy wants intimacy but does not know how to obtain this treasure. In this sad confession, we become aware of the spiritual poverty of JonBenet's mother. She is isolated from her unconscious, the seat of intuition. She is without friends. Her exterior life is resplendent with the accouterments of the upper class. Her interior life is hollow. There is no interior sun to keep her warm. As we proceed in this Spiritual Court of

Law (found in Chapter Eight, "Closing Arguments") investigation of the mother's psyche, we will grasp the magnitude of this woman's suffering.

Patsy forward, "God has a master plan for all of us and in the fullness of time our family will be united again and we will see JonBenet."

What a paradox. She mentions God and her psyche shouts this message: **We're running evil.**

Smoking gun number six. We have another confession of her wrongdoing. In her forward voice she talks about God. Her backward, authentic voice—the part of her that cannot lie—acknowledges she is being incongruent. In the lexicon of this technology, "incongruent" means lying and that the forward statement is inconsistent with the reversal. This creates disharmony between the conscious and unconscious. A state of dis-ease exists. This can result in a nervous breakdown that can lead to a spiritual breakthrough.

Yet another smoking gun

Patsy, forward, "…we have just basically read or watched very little. You can't. It's just overwhelming, we're grieving, and it's hurtful. I can't tell you how bad it is."

Her forward statement is honest, direct, simple and cuts to the essence of her suffering. The pain is genuine.

The psyche flashes two messages. **Yes, I did it. Spirit wolf bursting.**

The first reversal **Yes, I did it** amounts to *Smoking gun number seven* and is expressed with such emotion. She is scared that she will be convicted and sent to the gallows. On our Website you will be able to HEAR Patsy drag out and prolong the **Yes**.

Patsy's forward statement says "…It's just overwhelming, we're grieving, and it's hurtful. I can't tell you how bad it is." What she is unable to express in her forward voice explodes to the surface in the depth of her psyche. We understand the reason for her profound grief and suffering that torments her.

The second reversal decoded in this statement, **Spirit wolf bursting.**

Spirit refers to the totality of our being, the male and female aspects of our mind, where the male is the symbol of the intellect and female is the symbol of our intuitive self. This is another reference to the analogy Abraham Lincoln used about the house divided against itself cannot stand.

Cut off from her **spirit,** she is exiled in the wilderness, isolated in a barren country, starving in a spiritual wasteland. We create our heaven on earth and our hell on earth.

When the two revealing reversals are considered together, the intensity, duration and frequency of her suffering becomes staggering. Patsy Ramsey's heart is shredded, torn apart. While the heart continues to function on a physical level, the force behind the heart does not beat. Without a **spirit**, life is empty of joy.

In this technology, when **wolf** appears in a reversal, an alarm sounds, signaling very deep spiritual concerns, which can be healthy or disastrous, depending on the context. This is a powerful phrase of the psyche. When **spirit wolf bursting** appears in a reversal, a person is without any psychological armor or spiritual protection. This is a 911 call of distress. A Reverse Speech or Embedded Communication analyst understands the seriousness of the metaphor. The person is in immediate danger. A flying leaf in the air, the person's life has no direction, no control. The motivation for living is gone.

Patsy Ramsey requires immediate psychiatric help. If the help is not obtained, suicidal action can be taken. Or a plunge into drugs, alcohol, sexual activity or a myriad of other outlets will be attempted to ease the pain.

Singing the blues

The front cover displays a picture of JonBenet and the cowboy song she sang. Thanks to Gail Wilts relentless research, this song of Patsy Ramsey was discovered. Like her daughter's song, Patsy's tale also communicates the misery that plagues her.

Here are the words of the ditty sung by Patsy:

You say neither
I say neither
Either, either
Neither, neither
Let's call the whole thing off

Six messages are uncovered from the psyche. **Wrong at the heart. Fast and under. Evil number and each carry on yet dammit, try feeding ya.**

When a person sings a song that has been committed to memory, or practiced often, startling information is revealed. The reversals may not have anything to do with the forward statement. Instead, what the person is thinking or feeling during the singing is captured.

The psyche's communications are analyzed in segments. **Wrong at the heart.** Patsy's heart aches from the pain. Listening to the forward part of the song, we hear a lively ditty. The reversal takes us into Patsy's heart and we discover the upbeat quality crashes into moaning. Another paradox. Happiness and joy are portrayed by the persona, the concealing part of our self. The psyche or revealing aspect delivers an entirely different message.

Fast and under. Our interpretation is that the mother is thinking that the impending murder is about to take place or has recently occurred. The date when the song was song is unknown to us. **Under** suggest the body will be hidden for a while or concealed in a lower part of the house, like the basement.

Evil number. What a paradox we have stumbled upon. **Number** is another word for engaging in an activity as well as referring to a song. The song in her heart is an **evil number.**

And each carry on. In her emotions, thoughts and personality, she must **carry on** with her life.

Yet dammit, try feeding ya.

Patty is trying to show the public that she is a happy woman. **Dammit** illustrates how difficult it is to pull the act off—**try feeding ya.** Try as she might, her efforts are futile.

Additional Information

When the truth is spoken in the forward statement, the reversal may contain information that expands the original meaning. As we have seen from JonBenet's forward comment made in her cowboy song, her reversal shows she spoke the truth in addition to expanding her forward remark. In this example, what was bothering the child "surfaced" from the depths of her psyche.

Moving on, the Ramseys arranged a second CCN press conference. It was held in May 1997. Patsy makes the following statement, "We were just frantic and I immediately—I dialed the police. 911."

Two reversals are uncovered. **You sealed the bad here. You lady mannequin.**

JonBenet's death means the family's secret is safe—**sealed**—another term for locked away. Now no one will know that the child had been subjected to ongoing sexual abuse. Quieting her before she could make a public statement is a possible motive for the murder.

By unconsciously uttering **you lady mannequin** we are granted the privilege of exploring the mother's perception of the murdered child. A mannequin—the mother's reference to her daughter—is an object to be dressed up and paraded before the public. A mannequin has no feelings. It does not need love. A mannequin is something that is handled for one's benefit—to win beauty pageants for the mother and be exploited as a sexual object by the father. It indicates the de-humanization of the mother-daughter relationship.

In a way, the child became more of a person after her death. From the perspective of the mother, the corpse assumed life-like proportions.

A smoking gun

Patsy, forward, "I was out of my mind and it (the ransom note) said don't call the police, that type of thing."

The reversal, **Sealed the lock.**

Note that **sealed** was used previously, when Patsy said **you sealed the bad**. This confirms the mother's complicity in the murder. Smoking gun number eight. Another meaning is a description where the child was found—in a sealed room in the basement that was missed by the police in searches of the Ramsey home.

Patsy, forward, "I'd like to take a moment to just let you know how much we have appreciated the hundreds and hundreds of cards and letters and pictures that children have sent me, little angels and books, that wonderfully compassionate caring people from all over the world has sent to us…"

The reversal contains two messages. **Dad's myth was our promise. Soul wished mess.**

Forty-nine words were spoken forward. Eight in reverse. The "less is more" theme, as we shall see, becomes apparent once more. The two messages, delivered in a cryptic, telegraphic and compact fashion, require not a flashlight to illuminate the multiple meanings, but a spotlight. Once again, the unconscious takes center stage as we see the wonders contained in the depths of the iceberg.

The first reversal message, **Dad's myth was our promise.** This suggests that the wife and daughter were viewed as showpieces for the dad. In another ironic twist, Jon saw the two females in the family as mannequins. He married a former model (Patsy). His daughter became a showpiece by touring the beauty pageant circuit. They believed and followed him blindly. To please him, they subscribed to his myth. The mother's and daughter's **promise** of a wonderful life would be realized. From their perspective, Jon was the Pied Piper.

The message contained in the second part of the reversal results in her sorrowful revelation that toppled the dream into ruins. **Soul wished mess** is a prophecy that came true. Patsy ignored the repeated intuitive messages sent by her soul through recurring nightly dreams and daytime hunches. Stated another way, the intuitive message from her soul or the wisdom part of her being was ignored, resulting in complete chaos. This is not seen as a punishment from God in the form of divine retribution for the crime.

Rather, by not listening to the voice in her heart, Patsy set into motion events that have drowned her in sorrow.

Jon, forward, "...we received cards from Canada, Europe, certainly all of the United States. I have corresponded several times with a little girl..."

Jon's reversal, **I scared, sounding the lie loose.**

The father has plenty to be scared about. The sounds he makes in his verbal utterances contain the abundance of lies that have been set loose. David Oates, the founder and developer of this technology, posted many of Jon Ramsey's lies on his web site as early as January, 1998. The Reverse Speech analysts and students in the United States, Canada, Europe, Japan and other countries tape recorded the Ramseys' public statements on their Reversing Machines and sent them to the Reverse Speech website where David Oates posted the results. Public figures like President Clinton are aware that David Oates and the technology enthusiasts around the world share their findings on the website. In one of his reversals, President Clinton says the name of "Oates." Mark Fuhrman, in an interview on the Art Bell Show, mentioned "Oates" in one of his reversals. A government spokesman, when defending the downing of the ill-fated TWA flight 800, mentioned David Oates in a reversal.

Even though Jon Ramsey's conscious mind, as demonstrated in his forward comment, is not aware of the power of this awesome technology that unlocks the mysteries of the psyche, his unconscious mind is tuned into the reality. **I scared, sounding the lie loose** is an ominous warning that has come true. His ship is about to crash into the rocks that have been set loose by his lies.

What follows from Jon is another plunge into the depths of his psyche, revealing his sexual thoughts on pre-pubescent young girls. The father says, in his forward voice: "...it's just been wonderful, so we've come out of this perhaps differently than you would expect in believing that there really is a lot of goodness in the world. And that's been an outcome that I think we certainly wouldn't have anticipated with this kind of tragedy."

Four reversals are uncovered here.

Nice little girl. Let me look. Let me nurse you. You get down on my fire.

The first message comes from his dark side (the shadow). He is referring to his previous statement about corresponding "several times with a little girl." In his reversal, **nice little girl**, he is warming up for the fantasy that is about to occupy his mind. The fantasy takes an active role in his imagination, **let me look**. The assumption is that he is seeing her naked.

The third reversal expresses his desire, **let me nurse you**. He will take "good" care of the girl.

The fourth reversal, **you get down on my fire**, "gave me the chills," David Oates wrote when he decoded the unconscious message. In this glimpse into the father's dark side, we "see" him performing oral sex with the unsuspecting girl correspondent.

Jon Ramsey cannot hide his sexual secrets. An ironic twist took place in his forward statement when he used the word "tragedy." The tragedy continues to widen as additional information unfolds. His use of the word **fire** in his fourth reversal backfired on him. The sexual flame rages within him, creating an inferno that is out of control.

Returning to Patsy, forward she says, "…those were beautiful pictures, those, I'm so happy that we have them…"

The reversal, **Evil's answer.** Several layers of meaning are postulated from this seemingly bizarre response. One meaning has to do with the parents' motive for killing JonBenet. **Evil**—their crimes against the girl—was answered by silencing her. This is **evil's answer**. The sexual assault on the child, an evil act, was dealt with in an evil manner.

Here is another postulation. Up until now, JonBenet has been viewed as a tragic figure. She has been painted as an innocent child who was an unwilling victim. We are about to take an about face in describing JonBenet. With this out of the way, the mother looks into the "beautiful pictures" and sees the demonic face of JonBenet.

From the mother's view, the child was a bad seed that had to be destroyed. It was JonBenet, the seeming temptress, who lured her father into the sexual trap.

Again, from the mother's view, ridding the planet of a pestilence is an act that deserves admiration from the public, not blame and condemnation. A public ceremony should be held to celebrate their honorable act of putting evil to sleep. **Evil's answer.**

In the following segment, Jon Ramsey is seen as bitter. When the case comes to trial, he feels the cards are stacked against him. The trial can be a criminal proceeding or the reaction that results from the public's judgment of the evidence produced from the findings of the Spiritual Court of Law (see Chapter Nine, "Closing Arguments").

Jon, forward, says, "...at least up until yesterday anytime spent looking at us is time wasted and that in part is why we brought in an investigative team as well to immediately look in other directions."

The reversals are: **Do they love you. I was the drop man with her. I done it. It's a show you're running.**

From the father's perspective, the public has sympathy for his wife.

In the second reversal he sees himself as the pawn of his wife. **I was the drop man with her** indicates he did the murder. The responsibility for the crime has been **drop**ped on him. He feels if the case comes to trial there will be an outpouring of sympathy for his wife. Patsy will get off free in a criminal trial. He believes his fate is the gallows. Thus the bitterness alluded to in the opening statement of his statement.

The third reversal, **I done it** contradicts his previous reversal. This reflects his fragmented and disturbed mind. This is smoking gun number nine.

The fourth reversal reflects an earlier theme from the January 1997 CCN press conference. **It's a show you're running.**

A smoking gun

Patsy, forward, says, "...the ad that we placed in our local paper this weekend. This reward money has been offered since the death of JonBenet, but we felt like it wasn't got out to the public enough, so this ad with her most recent kindergarten picture will be featuring more frequently."

Two reversals here. **I know you've sinned. The soul we kill of you again.**

Smoking gun number ten. In addition to confessing to the crime, this unconscious disclosure indicates that the mother is pre-occupied with JonBenet's murder. "Peace be with you" is a foreign idea. **I know you've sinned.** With sin comes punishment. Day and night she is bombarded with thoughts that appear on the screen of her mind.

A verdict of guilty by a criminal trial jury would bring her comfort. Or an indictment from the Boulder, Colorado grand jury would be therapeutic. But the grand jury failed to issue an indictment in their decision that was made public in October 1999.

> **The soul we kill of you again.** This reflects the torture the mother undergoes daily. The second reversal complements the first reversal, creating smoking gun number eleven, a double confession in one statement.

It is time to announce that the author of *JonBenet Knows Evil Love* is claiming the reward money for finding information that will lead to the killers of JonBenet. Jon and Patsy Ramsey are accused of involvement of the murder of their child. Seventy-five percent of the money will go to further the research of this technology, promote research, finance one of the ongoing projects and set up a university program where students can be trained and certified in this exciting area.

On an unconscious level, she wants to be caught.

Forward Patsy says, "the police and investigators have assured us that this is a case which can be solved. You may be eluding the authorities for a time but God knows who you are and we will find you."

One telltale reversal. **They'll see your faith.**

On one level, God is mentioned to make sure the public is aware of her **faith**. On another level, she desperately wants the police to believe that the parents did not commit the crime. That is her prayer.

When the forward and reverse comments are viewed together, we see that Patsy Ramsey's mind is fragmented. President Lincoln said, "A house divided against itself cannot stand." A mind divided against itself cannot stand.

The New Testament tells us the alienation between the conscious and unconscious is a formula for disaster. "For he is our peace, who hath made both one, and hath broken down the middle wall or partition between us" (Ephesians 2:14). "He" is the Spirit that dwells within the sacred temple. "Made both one" is the conscious and unconscious or the male and female minds. When disconnected from the Source, a wall is built between the Spirit (God) and ourselves. This amounts to the creation of a Berlin Wall of the mind. Until that wall is bulldozed, Patsy Ramsey cannot know peace.

"What God has joined together, let no one take apart" (Matthew 19:6). When man, the conscious mind, and woman, the unconscious mind, are connected as one, peace and harmony reigns.

Jon Ramsey, forward, "...an arrest is absolutely necessary in our lives for closure."

The reversal, **Results, our warning.**

This is another ominous communication from the unconscious that the father is running scared. Like his wife, there is a cavernous gulf between his conscious and unconscious. No matter how careful he is, despite his attempts to elude capture by contaminating the crime scene evidence, he knows the cuffs will be slapped on his wrists.

Jon, forward, makes a personal statement to the killer during the May, 1997 CNN press conference. "We'll find you. We will find you. I have that as a sole mission for the rest of my life."

The reversal, **We now fool you.**

He needs to keep repeating the lie to convince himself of his innocence. In his heart he knows he is fooling or conning the public.

Once again, his forward and reverse statements reflect the precarious state of his mind. There is a collision between his conscious and unconscious. Forward, he tells us about his life long mission to seek out the killer. In reverse, the lie and deception surfaces from the depth of the iceberg. This is a page taken from O.J. Simpson who contends he will not be at peace until the killer of Nicole and Ron Goldman is caught and convicted.

Patsy, forward, "…we need that one phone call to this number that will help the authorities come to a conclusion to this case. Please, if you know anything, I beg you to call us."

Two reversals here. **Your man said it. So awkward.**

The first one indicates she and her husband had to work very hard to keep their story straight. This explains why the Ramseys insisted on being interviewed together by the police.

The second reversal complements the first. Indeed it was **awkward**.

A SMOKING GUN

Jon Ramsey forward, I want whatever resources I can bring to bare, brought to bare…"

Two reversals, one of them is a smoking gun number eleven. **Kill the source. That little crime messed up.**

The resources he intends to bring to the investigation are designed to serve as a smoke screen. Like O.J., he wants to show the American people his commitment to bring the killer to justice. The irony and double meaning of this message, **kill the source**, is that he, Jon Ramsey, is the source. He is killing himself. This will be discussed in "Closing Arguments."

That little crime messed up is smoking gun twelve.

Jon, "...we think we're a normal American family that loves and values their children."

The reversals, **Your life, a crime. Hormone.**

Jon's psyche takes exception that he loves and values his children with parental devotion. JonBenet, in her cowboy song, viewed this as **evil love.** To the Nazis, this is seen as Auschwitz love. From the viewpoint of the father's unconscious, his life is **a crime.** Smoking gun thirteen.

Hormone. One meaning is a chemical alteration in Jon. He lacks sexual control, as evidenced in the revealing reversals we uncovered in the little girl who corresponds with him. Those reversals are: **nice little girl; let me look; let me nurse you; you get down on my fire.**

Jon, forward, "...we think there's some very good people working on the case; we are very impressed that the people in the DA's office have brought in..."

The reversal, **repeat the nervous.**

Another warning from his unconscious. He is nervous and rattled about the genuine results that will point to him as the culprit.

Jon, forward, "...frankly for the first few months Patsy and I were really not capable of making any decisions."

Reversals, **Say yes again. We can.**

Psyching himself up.

Jon, forward, "...this was a process that the police went through with us as suspects. I don't believe any new information was provided that we hadn't provided very early on..."

Reversals, **They love it. Silly sham.**

He displays his contempt for the police and his arrogance. The press conference is staged to con the media and fool the public.

Jon, forward, "We had some initial reactions to who might have been involved."

Reversal, **Washing the slaves. Lost this new girl.**

Washing is a conscious attempt to cleanse themselves by pointing the finger at imaginary killers.

A possible meaning to **lost this new girl**—the father's fantasy over the young girl he was corresponding with did not become his new sex toy.

Patsy, forward, "It was difficult but they need to know, our handprints are all over our home."

Reversals, **Like my drugs. I rely on this.**

She turned to drugs to ease the difficult situation after JonBenet's death. She had to numb herself from her feelings.

The second reversal supports the first one.

Patsy, forward, "There is a killer on the loose…keep your babies close to you."

Reversals, **Feel the knot. We shock the memory.**

Patsy is tangled up—**Feel the knot**. She feels the knot in her stomach.

Try as she might, the mother is unable to rid her memory of the crime she committed. There is an uninterrupted unconscious communication from the wisdom part of herSelf to the ego part of the self. A spiritual current keeps jolting Patsy Ramsey. The drugs mentioned previously—**I rely on this**—does not accomplish its purpose, to numb her feelings and senses.

"Started in the basement and we're just looking and, we had one room in the basement."

Two reversals, **Search with them. Then he calls his unit.**

Jon is re-living the scene as he escorts the police. Aofter the unsuccessful search, the police contact headquarters in Boulder, Colorado.

This is a rare event. Jon Ramsey is telling the truth. His conscious mind (the ego) and his unconscious (the psyche) are in harmony.

Another confession

This chapter concludes with another confession/smoking gun statement communicated to Patsy Ramsey from her psyche. Forward, "America has just been hurt so deeply with this."

The revealing reversal, **Our crime.**

She has also been hurt. She senses that Americans know, at the unconscious level of mind, that she and her husband are responsible for the death of JonBenet.

Smoking gun fourteen.

Chapter Four

Highlights of the Technology on Our Radio Program

In this section we will provide some examples about this technology that appeared on our weekly program, Dance With Your Shadow, KEST 1450 on the AM dial. Gail Wilts, my research partner, co-hosted the show with me in the summer of 1998. We stopped the show when my agent told me that the JonBenet book would be published in a package. He suggested that we should write outlines for two more books on this technology. This turned out to be a false alarm.

Two skeptics call in

We will start off with two people who admitted they are skeptical about this technology. The first caller, George, was of the opinion that reversals contained gibberish and other manifestations of nonsense. If there was a coherent word or phrase, the result should be attributed to chance. If not attributed to chance, the result was accidental or coincidental. Either way, according to George our radio program, *Dance With Your Shadow* was doomed.

"George," I said, "you will be a blessing to our audience."

"That's not the way I see it, " he said. "It's obvious that I will be your Achilles heel."

"You mean your experiment with the Reversing Machine will be a cursing for the program instead of a blessing?"

"Exactly," George said. "Are you sure you want to experiment with me? My reversals will make skeptics of your believers."

"You're forgetting one thing George—"
I paused, waiting for him to respond.
"Cat got your tongue, Richard?"
"That's good, George. You forgot that your skepticism comes from your conscious mind."
"You're not going to give me that 'tip of the iceberg' nonsense, are you, Spiritual Outlaw? (my name on the show) You don't mind if I call you Spiritual Outlaw, do you?"
Other times, when we do the segment, "The Spiritual Court of Law," I am known as the Spiritual Assassin. My third name is Prayer Dog.
"Prayer Dog" comes from a Rumi poem called *Love Dogs*.

> One night a man was crying
> Allah! Allah!
> His lips grew sweet with the praising, until a cynic said,
> "So I have heard you calling out,
> but have you ever gotten any response?"
>
> The man had no answer to that. He quit praying and fell
>   into a confused sleep.
> He dreamed he saw Khidr, the guide of souls,
> "Why did you stop praising?"
> "Because I've never heard anything back?"
>
> "This longing you express
> is
> the return message."
>
> The grief you cry out from draws you toward union.
> …Listen to the moan of a dog for its master.
> That whining is the connection.

End of note. Back to George the skeptic. "It's your unconscious mind's opinion about this technology that we are seeking," I said.

"Okay, I'll go for that. What do you want me to do?"

"Tell us what you do in one sentence, George."

I made the "record now" gesture to Gail who was in the broadcast booth with me. She prepared the Reversing Machine for George's comment. Then she indicated that she had something to say before the statement was made. "George, this is Gail. Concentrate with an open heart on what you are about to tell us."

After a pregnant pause, George spoke as Gail released the pause button on the Reversing Machine.

The skeptic said, "My name is George and I teach salsa dancing."

Gail played the forward comment for George and the listeners to hear what the Reversing Machine recorded.

"My name is George and I teach salsa dancing."

Gail readied the "Doorway to the Psyche," the nickname of the device, for the playback.

She played the statement in reverse.

"All I hear is gibberish and static noise," George said.

This was true—to an extent. People new to the device usually hear only gibberish and alphabet fog. Sometimes there was no crystal clear reversal.

I watched Gail as she placed headphones on and deftly maneuvered the machine to different points. She was replaying George's comment at three different speeds, patiently listening for the Voice behind the voice to deliver its message to the Doubting Thomas.

This process took about two minutes. Meantime George maintained that nothing worthwhile would surface.

Gail flashed two hands up. She found something. Gleeful Gail removed the headphones. "George," she said, " I'll play your reversal. At the end of the gibberish you will hear two words delivered from your unconscious. Those words are **soooo silly**." She played the message. Gibberish and static noise penetrated the airwaves of San Francisco and the nine counties of the Bay Area.

Gail replayed the reversal. **Soooo silly.** George agreed that he heard the same words as Gail. He had no idea what the meaning was.

Gail told him the reversal occurred when he spoke his name.

"You mean that **soooo silly** occurred when I said 'George'?"

"Yes," Gail said.

"That proves it," George roared in a tone of triumph. "I don't think my name is silly."

If he was smirking, he had every right to be.

"Could it be," Gail said, "that you were thinking how silly you felt during the experiment?"

"Why, yes, that was exactly how I was feeling."

"George, this is the Spiritual Outlaw. "Remember what we've been saying on the program—this technology eavesdrops on the psyche."

"I'm overwhelmed," George said. "How is it done?"

The exact details mystified Gail and me. Even though we attended the Reverse Speech Convention and the workshops conducted by David Oates; even though we read all the literature on Reverse Speech and Embedded Communication; despite our spending time on listening to the playback, we were in the dark to offer an explanation of *why reversals occur.*

The second skeptic

The second person that identified herself as a skeptic asked to remain anonymous. We will call her Jessica. She called in July 17, 1998. Once again, Gail instructed her to open her heart and concentrate on what she was going to say.

"Ummm, ummm, I don't know what to say. Ummm, how are you?"

"That's perfect," Gail said.

"That's dumb," Jessica said. "I wanted to say something profound but I—"

"Your forward comment may have sounded trivial," I said. "Let's see the message your unconscious presented to you as a gift."

"I'm really embarrassed," Jessica said.

I watched Gail work with her headphones. She indicated I should go to a commercial. More time was needed to work on Jessica's reversal. I asked the skeptic to hold on and we would play the reversal as soon as Gail located it.

While the ads was being delivered I watched Gail at work. She was calm under this stressful situation of locating reversals, jotting down tell-tale syllables and re-playing the reversals. She listened on the headphones for consonants and vowel sounds as she concentrated on her Reversing Machine. She listened intently, then flashed a thumbs up gesture. She leaned over, pressed the mute levers on both of our mikes, and then asked me to take another minute of on-air time before getting to the reversals. "We're touching on metaphors in this one,." Gail said. She fixed the mute dials, returned to her place, pulled out the Metaphor Glossary and quietly turned the pages until she found what she was looking for.

During the improv time, I asked Jessica if she was still there. She said yes.

On the air, I said, "Jessica, did you hear what we found out with the skeptic last week?"

Thank God, she didn't tune in. I told her this was a good opportunity to review the findings of George. Like her, we had listeners who weren't with us last week.

When Gail gave me the thumbs up gesture, I re-played the **soooo silly** material.

Gail turned the mute button off her mike. "Jessica, this is what you said in your forward voice."

"That's embar—" Jessica began.

Before she could complete her word, the tape played her forward statement. "Ummm, ummm, I don't know what to say. Ummm, how are you?"

"You don't really expect to find anything in that, do you?" Jessica asked.

"Here's the reversal," Gail said. "**We always mock the aides. It's no wonder, that muck muck, is it?**"

"I'll play the reversals again, Jessica so you can hear what your unconscious came up with."

Gail replayed the reversals. "Even though it's played in reverse," Jessica said, I can recognize my voice but I have no idea what any of it means."

"Jessica," I said, "sometimes messages from the unconscious appear in symbols and images and can be cryptic and telegraphic in nature."

Gail took over and explained that multiple meanings are often contained in the mysterious language of the psyche. **Mock** means to deride or ridicule an idea that is new.

Jessica agreed she was mocking the technology, although she was astounded that her irrelevant and innocuous sentence contained this kind of material.

Once again, thoughts and feelings are brought to the surface, even though they are not expressed by the conscious mind. Unconscious material surfaces from our depths. We are more than we think we are. In Jungian and other depth psychology systems, this is known as making the unconscious conscious.

Her reversal, **We always mock the aides,** can represent both the technology, which is an aid to access the unconscious, as well as the Reverse Speech analysts who use this technology to detect hidden communications in human speech. Not only is the new technology ridiculed, the practitioners are also **mock**ed. Jessica accepted this interpretation.

Gail then focused on the second part of the reversal, **it's no wonder that muck muck.**

The caller was thinking that it was **no wonder** we always **mock the aides** that access the unconscious mind. The double **muck** emphasizes her belief that the technology is far-fetched or an aimless activity not worthy of serious study.

"Jessica," I said, "is Gail's interpretation too far out? Or is she right on?

"This is fascinating," Jessica said. "What I thought was irrelevant and—"

"Wait," Gail said, "there's more."

"What?"

"You ended with a question—how are you? Let me play your forward statement."

"Ummm, ummm, I don't know what to say. How are you?"

Gail told her reversal and then played it—**we always mock the aides. It's no wonder that muck muck, is it?**

"Your ending—**is it?**—poses a question," Gail said. "May I suggest what you meant?"

"By all means," Jessica said.

"The question in your reversal **is it?** reveals your possible acceptance of this technology in spite of your initial skepticism. While you think this technology is aimless activity and not worthy of serious consideration, you still have a nagging doubt and are receptive to this new technology that explores the iceberg below the conscious mind."

"It's true," Jessica said. "I'm ambivalent about this stuff. At the same time I find it fascinating."

From a skeptic to a true believer

My friend Mary Jane called the radio station to tell her story. She knew my involvement with Embedded Communication and wanted to share her experience with the audience.

The incident took place when I visited Mary Jane at her home. I brought the mini-Reversing Machine with me. Called the "YakBak," this device costs $18 and is available at most ToysRUs stores. You are able to record your forward comment up to seven seconds on the YakBak. When the "yalp" button is pressed, the YakBak plays the statement in reverse. Children love to play with the YakBak. They are tickled to hear themselves speaking backwards. The device is useful as a toy. It also serves as a mini-Reversing Machine.

At Mary Jane's home, I was introduced to her friend, Dottie. Her view on this technology was not given. Mary Jane declared herself a skeptic. Dottie's facial expression and demeanor indicated antagonism toward the thought that the unconscious could be captured on a machine. A camera can catch a physical picture. But a tape recorder coming up with information. Never.

I asked Mary Jane to speak into the YakBak, preferably with emotion.

Without any hesitation, Mary Jane burst out, "I think Richard Rubacher is crazy."

The reversal contained gibberish. Toward the end, in a clear voice, we heard **he's a picnic.**

Mary Jane, incredulous, pressed the Yalp button again to hear her forward statement and the reversal. **He's a picnic** "Richard," she said, "that's what I think of you. You're fun to be with."

I asked Dottie if she heard **he's a picnic.** She nodded. I asked if she would like to say something. No way.

Mary Jane, puzzled, marveled at the outcome. "My God, how can that be? I said something forward and the answer came back with something I was thinking."

"Your thoughts," I said, "are picked up and carried into your speech."

Mary Jane asked me to show Dottie the Shakespeare quote and T.S. Eliot's insight into the hidden messages contained in our speech.

> *His forward voice, now, is to*
> *speak well of his friend; His*
> *Backward voice is to utter.*
> *Foul speeches and to detract.*

"Richard, tell Dottie when Shakespeare said that."
"AD 1611."
"And what did T.S. Eliot say?"
"The word behind the word."
"When did he say that?"

"In 1920."

"And along came this guy in the 1980s. What's his name?"

"David Oates."

Mary Jane nudged her friend. "Go on, Dottie, yack into the YakBak."

"No way, MJ."

Mary Jane took the YakBak and burst out, "You cannot reverse anything with this technology."

Then she played it forward to make sure the recording took. Then backward. The reversal said, **now we can.**

Mary Jane could not restrain her awe and fascination with the YakBak. She nudged Dottie, encouraging her to try it out.

"No way, MJ."

"Go on, it won't bite you."

"Yes it will, MJ."

Then the reason for Dottie's reluctance came out. A frequent listener of the radio program, Dottie referred to the disclaimer statement we made on a regular basis.

The disclaimer: "We want to point out that we cannot play a reversal over the air when you call in with a puzzling dream or nightmare or voice a genuine concern. The answer may be dreadful or wonderful. You may faint over the phone. You may dig up shameful material about your relationship or family secrets may surface. You may also find yourself using offensive language that may jeopardize the radio station with the Federal Communications Commission."

Dottie confessed that two, three or four of the dreadful outcomes would surface from her psyche.

"No way, MJ, will I yak into that dreadful machine."

Mary Jane's nine-year-old daughter Molly came home from school. She couldn't wait to hear the O.J. Simpson reversals. Her mother promised that I would include the Judge Ito-O.J. exchange.

"From day one of the trial," Molly said, "I knew that O.J. was the murderer. I can't wait to hear his confession and what Judge Ito said."

Molly asked if it would be okay for some of her friends to hear the O.J. reversals.

When I gave the thumbs up gesture, Molly jumped with joy. "Come on in, guys," she said.

Four of her schoolmates popped into the room.

He wants to know if God is with him

Back at the radio station, Gail took a phone call from a Native American shaman (a healer). He requested a session on the YakBak. A frequent listener, he was aware that his request should be seven seconds or less. For a longer statement the full-scale Reversing Machine is needed.

"When I reach 'one,' Gail said over the airwaves, "talk from your heart."

"Three, two, one."

On cue, he said, "Is God with me?"

Gail released the "play" button on the YakBak.

"Is God with me?" the healer said in his forward voice.

"Get ready for the playback in reverse," Gail said.

"I'm ready."

Him so proud of thee.

Both of us in the studio were stunned. We were on the air with a holy man.

"Are you still on the line?" Gail asked.

"Yes, ma'am."

"Let me play it again."

Him so proud of thee.

"Richard will talk to you while I look something up. I think the results will astound us."

Gail consulted her Metaphor Dictionary while I chatted with the caller.

"Sir—" I said. Gail cut me off.

"Listen to this," she said. "I'm quoting from the Metaphor Dictionary. THEE, from old English; a term of respect; adds great emphasis to a reversal."

"It is as though God is bowing in respect to you," I said.

"What an honor to hear the voice of the spirit," the Native American said. "I thank you so much."

After he hung up, Gail pointed out that the healer was in touch with the cosmic and transcendental dimensions of his being. How true.

An experiment to trick the unconscious by lying

One of the most challenging questions came from a woman listener through Dance With Your Shadow email. "Can you lie and not have it detected in the reversal?" was her question. Gail and I found her challenge intriguing. Can we fool the unconscious by stating a deliberate lie in a forward statement?

We would perform a simple experiment by telling a blatant lie, then play it backwards and hear the results. Would the answer topple this technology from its foundation? Would we discover that Reverse Speech is a fraud? I would go first, then Gail would take her turn.

No matter what happened, we would broadcast the results on the next program of *Dance With Your Shadow.*

Instead of lying I would ask a question whose answer I already knew.

Here is the background and the reason I posed this question. James F. Files, in his 1993 confession, stated that he was the man on the grassy knoll on that fateful day in Dallas. He confessed he shot the fatal blow that killed John F. Kennedy Jr. In my forward voice, I said, "I don't know which Psalm applies to the JFK killer."

The reversal, **I lick yes. Pay through the self. Moss, get one, oh yea.**

I lick means to explore, to check something out. That is true, I was exploring the issue. But not really, because I was lying.

Pay through the self. One meaning was that the correct Psalm number had already been to me—**pay through the self**. My unconscious delivered the answer to my conscious self.

The third part of the reversal contained surprising information. The Metaphor Dictionary (compiled by David Oates) states this about **moss:**

"The influences of the past, sometimes beneficial, sometimes not." The unconscious stretched the word out. M-o-s-s. It was telling me that I had previously dealt with this concern in the past (four months ago).

When the puzzle was pieced together, I learned that my unconscious tricked me.

Instead of telling me I was lying, it reminded me that the issue was resolved.

The experiment proved that I was not able to trick my deeper Self.

More background is needed to clarify what is going on. I was involved in Reverse Speech research project. James F. Files, the alleged killer of JFK, spoke at length about his role with the Chicago Mafia. I listened to the extensive Reverse Speech CD and tapes. Files expressed no remorse over his assignment to assassinate then-President Kennedy. What impressed me about his reversals was his constant referral that only he and God witnessed the execution. Like O.J. Simpson and the Patsy Ramsey, Files' unconscious showed he was troubled about executing JFK. He made—in his reversals—seven references to the Psalms. I wanted to get a message to him in his prison cell in the Joliet State Prison in Illinois where he is serving a life sentence for killing an Illinois law enforcement officer. Not knowing which Psalm would comfort him, I posed the question to the YakBak. "Which Psalm applies to the alleged killer of JFK?"

The playback was ninety-five percent incomprehensible gibberish. The last two words were: Psalm 6. I immediately turned to that Psalm. To my astonishment, Psalm 6 was the spiritual medication that James F. Files needed.

The next experiment focused on Gail. I would ask her to attempt lying to the eternal part of herSelf.

Our second experiment to trick the unconscious

Gail Wilts, center stage please.

To make the test more difficult for the unconscious, Gail decided to tell a *lie* and a *truth* in the question she would pose to her psyche.

"My name is Janet Wilson and I am forty-eight years old," Gail Wilts said into the Reversing Machine.

To make sure the Machine captured the lie and truth, I re-played her forward statement. "My name is Janet Wilson and I am forty-eight years old."

As we know, the lie is found in the forward statement. Her name is not Janet Wilson. The truth is that she was forty-eight years old.

With a sense of dread and awe, we listened to the long reversal. The Voice behind the voice of Gail Wilts spoke.

Four three Gail, age missed low, do me now.

We had to break the reversals down into multiple sections and decipher each part separately. Only then could we solve the mystery of this puzzling response.

Four-three. Gail is forty-eight, not forty-three. Bad news and we only just begun.

The next reversal, **Gail,** showed us that her unconscious corrected her name. Good news mixed in with the bad.

Age missed low. After much scratching of our heads, the light went on. Her unconscious relayed the news that it deliberately gave a younger **low age.** That is, **four-three** instead of four-eight.

While Gail and I were trying to trick her unconscious, it turned out the unconscious played a trick on us. Deep within us is a child at play.

Do me now. An obvious reference to sex. Gail was thinking of sex when she posed her question.

"Not true," Gail protested. "I didn't have sex on my mind during the experiment."

She said I was projecting. I played the **do me now** portion of the revealing reversal back, not once, not twice, but a bunch of times.

Do me now. Do me now. Do me now.

"Okay, Richard, okay. You're right. It is **do me now.** You drilled it into me."

"Gail, did you hear what you just said?"

"Yes, you drilled it into me."

"Drilled is another sexual innuendo. This time the sexual imagery came in your forward voice."

"Richard, you're telling me that consciously and unconsciously I had sex on my mind?"

Sex and the unconscious

Sex plays a powerful role in our conscious and unconscious. David Oates appears to have struck a vital note when he penned this in his Metaphor Dictionary. "Sex is what makes it all work."

The Metaphor Dictionary continues:

According to this technology, the unconscious mind sees Sex as fuel that drives the human engine. Sex therefore is any form of high energy that keeps it all going; in the positive sense, Sex can be power, money, business, relationships, and connection. Sex can also be depression, anger, sabotage, etc.; whatever the unconscious has gotten used to as normal stimulation.

Lick, another sexual metaphor commonly found in reversals, is a delightful and colorful method of expression that characterizes the unconscious.

To connect softly; to flirt; to pursue a new contact further; to explore; to check something out. See Touch and Kiss.

The following day, after she had a chance to sleep on the sexual disclosure, Gail told me that her reversal said **doobie now.**

"Good try," I said.

Enter Mark Fuhrman

One day Gail announced in an excited manner that Reverse Speech had found Mark Fuhrman innocent of wrongdoing in the Trial of the Century. David Oates' website contained reversals from Fuhrman's interviews with Geraldo on his television show and the Art Bell radio broadcast where the ex-detective appeared as a guest of Art Bell. Gail suggested that *"Dance*

With Your Shadow "call the former detective and perjurer onto the witness stand for one of our "Spiritual Court of Law" segments.

To me, Mark Fuhrman was resolved. It did not need exhumation. My mind was closed. I found Fuhrman guilty of deception and blatant lies from watching him on the witness stand. Like many of us, I thought that O.J. would have been convicted in the criminal trial if Fuhrman did not testify.

"You've got to hear his reversals," Gail said. "A perjurer is one who lies," she continued. "Don't you want to hear his reversals?"

Why not.

Before listening to his unconscious revelations on the Reverse Speech website, I watched the video of Geraldo interviewing Fuhrman. I was convinced that Geraldo's confrontational style would make the former detective crumble before the verbal onslaught of mighty Geraldo. Even a tough dude like Alan Dershowitz could not withstand the wrath of Geraldo, who knows how to play the menacing ogre. It was unbelievable to see Alan Dershowitz cower to Geraldo. Never had I seen Dershowitz as a humble, mild-mannered, soft-talking man. Dershowitz spoke with true reverence. It was as though a king had summoned one of his lowly subjects. My respect for Geraldo's power reached to the heavens and beyond.

I turned the Geraldo-Fuhrman video on, expecting the warrior of the airwaves to demolish Mark Fuhrman with ease. Instead, the ex-detective deflected the verbal thrusts of the attorney-trained television mega-star. The soft-spoken, boyish charm that characterizes the perjurer created an impact on Geraldo. The TV host softened his style. He stopped attacking his guest. He actually *listened* to his guest. Gone was the pit bull snarl. There was a softness, a gentleness in Geraldo's manner that I had never seen. His softness and responsiveness elevated him in my mind.

When the show ended I was confused about the *real* Mark Fuhrman. Did this man with the choirboy face and easy laugh trick the mighty Geraldo and con him?

It was time to end my confusion. By listening to Fuhrman's reversals I was ready to meet the *real* Mark Fuhrman.

The former detective, forward, "Yes, we were trying to make a screenplay, and it was fun."

He was talking about his use of the "N word," explaining that he used it when he wrote the script ten years prior to the Trial of the Century. In the script he made repeated references to the "N word" in addition to creating fictional scenes that characterizes feature films. The purpose of repeating the word was to portray the fictional character as a racist.

Fuhrman's reversal, **aw damn it.**

This meaningful reversal shows that he was in a Catch-22 situation. Nothing he could say about writing a script ten years ago would apply to the dilemma he faced in the courtroom. The DreamTeam displayed an uncanny ability to make it appear to the jury—and the worldwide television audience—that an event that took place years ago was happening now in Furhman's life. The DreamTeam's strategy worked. The "N word" came out during the trial as racial slurs, not as fictional characters speaking lines in a Hollywood film.

Thanks to Geraldo's relentless pursuit, Fuhrman's interrogation was taken to another level. Fuhrman was asked to explain his reason for not informing Marcia Clark and the other members of the prosecution team about his repeated use of the word.

Fuhrman, forward, "It was a screenplay. Why should I worry about this? It's not something I would hold guilt for. It's not like a true life experience." Fuhrman's reversals, **Not guilt, like walking around in the sunset.**

He believes the use of the word in the script was not a sign of guilt, or, as his psyche stated in the reversal, **not guilt.** In his mind, composing the screenplay was as innocent an activity as **walking around in the sunset.**

Fuhrman, forward, "The city (Los Angeles) and the world started making a big deal about a professional testimony I gave, something I'd been doing for twenty years."

His reversal, **whirlwind innocent.**

David Oates wrote this about the reversal. "This reveals what he felt about his testimony. This is the same testimony that the city and the world was attempting to use to show that he was a liar and therefore, none of his testimony could be trusted."

The reversal **whirlwind innocent** David Oates continues, "is very meaningful because the word 'whirlwind' means with all your being."

David Oates concludes with the statement, "Fuhrman really believes he is innocent, or **whirlwind innocent.**"

The Metaphor Dictionary describes *Whirlwind* as an "energy that radiates out from the body to interact with the whirlwind of the cosmos; God's light travels the whirlwinds."

On the radio show, we played five more statements of Fuhrman followed by the reversals. The presiding spiritual judges (Rubacher and Wilts) in the courtroom at the radio station in San Francisco found Mark Fuhrman innocent of any wrongdoing (perjury) in the Trial of the Century. We asked the spiritual judges assembled around their radios to cast their verdict in accordance with the information accessed from the unconscious of the accused.

The conclusion we reached from hearing the case in the Spiritual Court of Law is that the defense deserved the name given them by the media—the DreamTeam.

Another conclusion we reached was stated previously, where we speculated that Judge Ito's finding O.J. Simpson guilty may have resulted in the judge's leaning over backwards during the trial to favor the defense team. To prove that a fair trial was being conducted, the judge allowed an avalanche of irrelevant testimony, including the introduction of the "N word" from the defense. The judge permitted defense witnesses to be repeatedly harangued by the prosecution team. Remember Barry Check taunting the police crime lab technician, Mr Fung?

In his own mind, Judge Ito felt guilty about pronouncing the defendant guilty by delving below the tip of the iceberg and into the

unconscious mind of the fallen football hero. As we have seen earlier, Judge Ito, in his unconscious dialogue with O.J. said you killed them. Simpson's response from his psyche, I skinned them, Judge Ito violated his professional code of ethics which declares the magistrate remains impartial during the proceedings.

Chapter Five

The Ramseys Second Fatal Flaw —They Talk Again

Part One: The Ramseys Second Fatal Flaw—They Talk Fifteen Months Later

Part Two: The Larry King Show and the Damaging Reversals of Patsy's Sister

The British-made documentary was cablecast in the United States on October 13, 1998. Gail Wilts and I spent a week analyzing the tape for reversals. The first thing we noticed was the psychological transformation of Patsy Ramsey from the early 1997 CNN press conferences. In 1997 Patsy was an emotional cripple from guilt feelings and suffering from melancholia over her involvement in JonBenet's murder. She required the "Doestoevsky medicine" —to confess her crime in order to save her soul from further anguish. The 1998 British documentary shows that Patsy

Ramsey has a frozen heart. **This bitch did it,** she said in the voice of her unconscious (referring to the ransom note authored by Patsy).

As the interview unfolded, we discovered that Patsy became the boss in the Ramsey household. When she disliked the answers that Jon was feeding the interviewer she effectively cut him off and took the responsibility to answer the question "correctly." In her reversal, Patsy's unconscious spoke in a *male voice.* Gail and I thought that her husband had interjected something and it was his voice that we heard. This proved to be wrong when we compared his previous reversals to the new male voice. Then we suspected that the male interviewer, Mike Tracy, made the comment while Patsy spoke.

By comparing the voice of the interviewer's unconscious, we realized that the masculine voice was not his either. Lo and behold, the man's voice belonged to Patsy Ramsey. What better way to show that she had assumed control of the story line than to speak in a masculine voice that carried authority. This was the first time in our experience with Reverse Speech and Embedded Communication that a person's unconscious spoke in the opposite sex.

We then studied the difference in Jon Ramsey's personality during the time period from the last CNN press conference (May 1997) to the British documentary (October 1998). Jon's change involved his being more scared than before. He was afraid of being tried and convicted of his daughter's murder. We discovered the first Freudian slip **I walked downSCARES.** He meant to say downstairs.

We checked out the interviewer's attitude toward the guests for his unconscious feelings on the parents' guilt or innocence. Mike Tracy, a professor at the University of Colorado at Boulder, did not commit himself either way on this question. The interviewer saw himself as the mythological Greek hero who is on a journey to find the truth about the Ramseys. He became frustrated because he felt that he did not find the truth. *However,* by placing himself as an advocate, he succeeded in putting the Ramseys at ease. By not barking at them with hostile questions, and by not being confrontational, Mike Tracy enabled the Ramseys to reveal far more than they intended to.

More smoking guns were found in the British documentary. They are identified in the analysis.

The voice of JonBenet is heard again, when a videoclip is played. The meaning of "evil love" is expanded. JonBenet senses that something dreadful is about to occur.

The chapter concludes with several comments made by Patsy's sister, Pam Paugh, on the *Larry King Show* that was cablecast on October 19, 1998. Through the voice of her psyche, Pam Paugh believes that the Ramseys are involved in JonBenet's murder.

The British documentary on the Ramseys

Jon, "The American public has been led to believe that while we went to bed that night before Christmas, brutally beat JonBenet, sexually molested her, strangled her, then went to sleep, got up the next morning, wrote a three-page ransom note, called the police, sat around the house for four hours, then I went downstairs (Freudian slip, he said "down-scares" instead of downstairs) and discovered her body. Help me understand that."

Six reversals appeared. First, I've answered none of your points. This is his response to the interviewer asking about the state of mind of the Ramseys when JonBenet's body was located.

The second reversal. **So I remember that I sealed the book on.** This indicates finality. **Sealed the book**—the work was completed.

The third reversal. **Go on up the stairs and yea leave the note.** Referring to the ransom note written by his wife.

The fourth reversal. **And you know whose skin that I feel still.** He is re-living the crime when JonBenet was murdered. Smoking gun fifteen.

The fifth reversal. **Yield her bod.** That is, surrender JonBenet's body to the police. The second meaning is to give up a habit—no more sex with his daughter.

The sixth reversal. **That night was hell. We wound the deal/you'll want the garbage.** He is telling us that the American public has been led to believe that while we went to bed and that someone entered the house and killed JonBenet.

Hell. A period of emotional turmoil for Jon and his wife. The agony is self-created. Smoking gun sixteen.

We wound (concluded) **the deal. Deal**—to take care of the problem by winding it up.

You'll want the garbage. The present interviewer and the British and American public are getting more garbage.

A videoclip of JonBenet rolls. Once again, she is dressed in a scanty outfit. She sings, "Yeehaw, I can sing away. I want to be a cowboy singer."

There are two reversals. **Mommy sad.** JonBenet is picking up her mother's vibrations.

JonBenet's second reversal. **Mommy, could I hear a terror in this kindness?** She is asking her mother if there is something awful in her father's love for her.

During the documentary another videoclip of JonBenet appears. Once again, she sings the cowboy song. This time she adds: "I want to learn to rope and ride."

JonBenet's reversal: **I had a naked body and now I hide.** She feels ashamed of what's going on with her dad. She is trying to bury the bedroom scenes from her mind.

The interviewer to Jon: "Did you have anything to do with the death of JonBenet?"

Jon Ramsey, "No, we did not."

His reversal. **And I'd be the one.** Smoking gun seventeen.

Background information. Jon Ramsey is talking about helping his son Burke who is building a model toy. This is the night of the murder. Mom already put JonBenet to bed. He told of the family's plan to travel to Michigan the day after Christmas. "And leave to go to Michigan in the morning. So I helped him put it together (the model) so I could get him to go on to bed."

Multiple reversals are found here. **Mad night. I had the note and anything else related. Look. With my house. Make it sham bogus.**

He's playing to the audience; it's a show he's putting on. He feels he has the sympathy of the viewers. He has the viewers in the palm of his hands.

House means the totality of his mind. All his attention was focused on the killing.

...I had the note Smoking gun eighteen.

He refers to the ransom note again: "I kind of turned around, looked at it to see what it was."

The long reversal: **And it's now but obvious that I had looked and I have nursed that** (**nurse,** to nurture, to help grow. He was in on the ransom note). Smoking gun nineteen.

Patsy is talking. "It just kind of wasn't registering that somewhere it said we have your daughter" (the ransom note says the kidnappers have JonBenet).

Her reversals. **God, remeyou, Messy, you're real messy. Nurse in there** (spoken in a male voice) **The winner. This bitch did it.**

As discussed in the opening remarks of this chapter, Patsy has become hardened in the heart. Her guilt has dissolved. She is calling the tune these days. She gloats over her new-found power (**the winner**).

This bitch did it. Smoking gun twenty.

In the conversation, Patty tells the interviewer that she and her husband are wondering what to do. She is referring to the ransom note that stated they are not to involve the police. The note said "if you even talk to a stray dog, she dies."

Her reversal. **I had need to swab the seal, maybe. Swab**—to hide the evidence before contacting the police. **Seal**—to protect them from being found out. Smoking gun twenty-one.

Patsy to the interviewer, about what to do. (Patsy sighs) "Send somebody over here quickly, you know."

Her reversals. **Bloody, you feel free. Who are you? I'm a friend, friend.**

You feel free. This demonstrates yet again that Patsy is no longer guilt-ridden. Since the CNN interview 15 months ago, she has come to terms with the crime. She is hardened.

Who are you? She is a changed person, psychologically-hardened.

She then answers her question: **I'm a friend, friend.** She accepts the dark side of herself (her shadow). She is engaging in a dialog with her shadow.

What follows is a continuation of the last dialog.

Patsy, "I couldn't get it out fast enough, you know."

Her reversals. **Finally find a part. That's why I did it. New scum.** Refers to the new-found ally, her shadow. **Scum,** a message from the wisdom part of herself. She must look into her motives. **Scum**—the dialog of the good and evil side of her personality continues to be heard.

Jon Ramsey. "It probably rang a half a dozen times and it was always (somebody else). But every time it rang, why my heart would stop."

Jon's reversals. **I see no perfume (gibberish). We must give it up. Sly animus.**

Perfume to sweeten and heal and alter or disguise the evidence in addition to present himself in a perfumy manner. He must give up his sexual attraction to young girls. He will be caught if he continues to have sex with pre-pubescent girls. His ongoing fear haunts him.

Sly animus. He is screwing JonBenet on the **sly. Animus** in the Reverse Speech Lexicon refers to the male energy, in this case, semen.

Jon Ramsey. "Her eyes were closed. I feared the worst. But yet I found her."

Jon's reversals. **Very mild yup baggage. Sure was nervous. Looked bizarre.**

He sees the body of his dead daughter as **baggage.** He was **nervous.** He is about to carry JonBenet's body to the police who are waiting upstairs. Will his **bizarre** story be believed?

Jon Ramsey. "And she was back in our safe (protection again)"

The reversal. **Awaken a shadow.** He is experiencing the dark side of himself when he used JonBenet as his sex toy. This is another lie to fool the interviewer, the British and the American public. His so-called protection consisted of sexually molesting his daughter.

The interviewer talks to Susan Stine, a neighbor of the Ramseys in Boulder, Colorado. Susan Stine. "None of us could imagine how this could have happened?"

Susan Stine's reversal. **Look what happened?** (two gibberish words). **The sham.**

She thinks Patsy is putting on a show.

Jon Ramsey's friend, Mike Bynum, told him that he needed legal counsel. "What in the world for?" Jon said to the interviewer.

Jon Ramsey's reversal. **Yes, and I am the one.** The reversal indicates that Jon knew he needed counsel because he was guilty. Smoking gun twenty-two.

Jon immediately follows this with, "We began to realize we are suspects. I was okay with that because I assumed it was a broad investigation."

The Ramseys' attorney, Bryan Morgan, talks to the interviewer. "It is foolish to blindly throw oneself into the law of the justice system."

The attorney's reversal. **I smell wolf. He'll meow.**

Smell. The attorney is assessing the situation (**smell**ing it out). **Wolf** is the prime motivation behind behavior. The state of Jon Ramsey's **wolf** is "cat-like" (**he'll meow**), which means that Jon Ramsey is deceptive, elusive, devious, would not let anyone close; very centered on self; will give affection when it serves his purpose. *The attorney is describing, at the unconscious level, his client's personality.*

The interviewer say to Jon, "So you have by this time begun to conclude that people were beginning to point the finger at you."

Jon, "We were hearing that from our friends.

Jon's reversal. **I'm hearing through you.** He's acknowledging that his friends are doubtful of his innocence.

Patsy, "I hadn't heard any of that and (like I say) I was in really bad shape."

On the TV she is emotional, waving her husband to keep quiet. She realizes he blew it by what he said. In her mind Patsy sees the deluge coming.

Patsy's reversal. **Yes, I be heard and this is the riot and here it comes.**

She states that one of her friends said that people are talking about her and Jon being involved in JonBenet's death. Her friend doesn't want Patsy to be upset.

"The friends say, "I'm going to tell you this and I don't want you to get upset. But they're saying and it's being reported that you and Jon may have been involved in JonBenet's death."

Patsy's reversal. **I've been emotionally involved in it, right.**

This is followed by another revealing reversal. **Oh I done it.** Smoking gun twenty-three.

The documentary cuts to the mayor of Boulder. She is upset about Patsy's statement in the CNN interview that a child killer is on the loose in Boulder.

"People in Boulder have no need to fear that there is someone wandering the streets of Boulder have been portrayed by, um, some people."

The mayor's reversal. **The answer, they miss it. That you're involved with fears and you're involved.** The Mayor believes the press blew up out of proportion that a killer is on the loose **the answer, they miss it.**

The mayor is adamant that Patsy is creating hysteria by her comment and is responsible for creating an atmosphere of **fear.**

Not only is Patsy **involved** in trying to create the unpleasant atmosphere, she is also **involved** in the death of JonBenet.

Cut to Patsy who responds to the mayor's comment. Patsy. "I don't know why she said that. And to this day I don't know why she said that."

Patsy's reversal. **I love this show.** She is proud of her power to influence the community. She feels grandiose. On another level, Patsy is ecstatic about the tone of this documentary and how easy it is to manipulate the English producers. More contrived than a movie. She loves that A&E and English producers of the documentary are favorable to her and are buying her version.

Cut to the mayor who is sitting with the interviewer. She has seen Patsy's response and is asked to reply. The mayor, "The information that I had at that time was that we did not have some crazed person (in the community of Boulder)."

The mayor's reversal. **And the sham.** The mayor thinks that Patsy is putting on a show in this documentary. The mayor has been consistent in her assessment of the Ramseys.

The documentary continues with Patsy responding to the interviewer's question that the parents killed JonBenet.

Patsy, "That's absolutely absurd."

Her reversal. **I feel the sweat.**

Sweat—a term for the scent of sexual attraction. Patsy is aware of her husband's sexual attraction to JonBenet.

The documentary cuts to Patsy talking about the day at the supermarket when her son saw the tabloid article that accused the parents of murdering JonBenet.

Patsy, "He was blank and he just sort of looked away…"

Patsy's reversal. **It's no accident.**

She confesses that the killing was **not accident.** Smoking gun twenty-four.

The interviewer asked Patsy to comment on the report in the tabloids that the parents killed JonBenet because of a bed-wetting problem.

Patsy, "It is so minuscule compared to me going through advanced ovarian cancer."

She emphasizes "so."

Patsy's reversal. **Oh, us did it.** Smoking gun twenty-five.

The interviewer, Mike Tracy, professor at the University of Colorado: "Did you ever consider each other?"

The interviewer's reversal. **I lost Ulysses.** The interviewer sees himself as the mythological Greek hero who is on a journey to find the truth about the Ramseys. He is frustrated because he has not found the truth. *However,* by placing himself as an advocate, he succeeded in creating a favorable atmosphere that allowed Jon and Patsy to be more spontaneous than they were in the CCN press conferences.

Jon Ramsey answers "No."

Patsy says, "Absolutely not."

Jon's reversal. **One.**

Patsy's reversal. **And you lose that one.**

This is the first three-way conversation that was located in the ninety minute documentary. Their unified front is effective as they are speaking as one.

Jon Ramsey, "…would have given our life for JonBenet."

Jon's reversal. **Hear the monster. Monster**—from the Metaphor Dictionary: "Deeply repressed energies or emotions lurking in the depths of unconsciousness." Also means "one's deepest fears."

Hear is to understand one's deepest fears.

The **monster** is the secret behind the words Jon Ramsey. This shows that he continues to be haunted by JonBenet in the same way that O.J.'s unconscious gnaws at him.

Jon Ramsey, "To protect her I would have given my life for JonBenet."

Jon's reversal. **Hear the monster, well um. Good whoppers. Precipice.**

Once again, the name of JonBenet evokes a deep fear in the father—the fear of being caught. **Precipice.** He realizes they are on the brink of disaster. It is essential they concoct an air-tight story. To accomplish this they must resort to **good whoppers.**

Larry King's interview with Pam Paugh, Patsy Ramsey's sister.

This interview was cablecast on CNN on October 19, 1998, seven days after the British documentary appeared on the A&E Network. Larry King asked Pam Paugh if the Governor of Colorado should clear her sister and brother-in-law's name. She said no because they haven't done anything wrong, "and I can appreciate that."

Pam's reversal. **Yes, sure, he's done it.**

Larry King asks if she would inform on the Ramseys if she knew they were involved in JonBenet's murder. She insists she would blow the whistle because she loved JonBenet.

Pam Paugh, "Family is family."

Her reversal. **You'll mask it. You'll miss.**

The sister has no intention of turning her flesh and blood in. **You'll mask it.** She is smug that the American public and the media will continue to be kept in the dark.

Chapter Six

The Bible, Shakespeare, & T.S. Eliot Know It

Before the breakthrough of this technology in 1983, the only evidence for the existence of a voice behind the voice came from the intuitive understanding of such literary giants as T.S. Eliot and Shakespeare. The divinely inspired prophets and sages in the Old Testament who wrote the Psalms, Book of Proverbs and the Book of Job also had a grasp of the "voice behind the voice." The New Testament reference to "the other Voice" is found the fourth gospel of Saint John.

T.S. Eliot & this technology

Traveling backward in time, we find a reference to the secret language of the soul in the writings of the poet, T.S. Eliot. In 1920, Eliot wrote these words in Gerontion: the word behind the word.

Shakespeare & Reverse Speech technology

In 1611, the bard penned these words in The Tempest, Act II, Scene II

> His forward voice, now is to
> speak well of his friend; His
> backward voice is to utter
> foul speeches and to detract.

The Bible contains multiple references to the hidden voice within. First we will look at the New Testament.

> In the beginning was the Word, and the Word was with God, and the Word was God.
> —John 1:1 King James Version

"Word" is capitalized, indicating what we say is sacred, or intended to be sacred. As we have seen in the Introduction, while we can lie in our forward voice, the sacred voice of the soul or psyche speaks the truth at all times.

> And the Word was made flesh.
> —John 1:14 King James Version

That is, the soul descended into matter, sanctifying the flesh.
Let us examine the Old Testament.

> Your own mouth condemns you, not mine. Your own lips testify against you.
> —Job 15:6 Living Insights Bible

> Your own lips bear witness against you.
> —Job 15:6 King James Version

> Not a word from their mouth can be trusted;
> their heart is filled with destruction,
> their throats are wide-open graves,
> their tongues seductive.
> —Psalm 5:9 New Jerusalem Bible

> You curse and you lie and vile language streams from your mouth
> —Psalm 52:4 King James Version

> He will turn their own tongue against them and bring them to ruin.
> —Psalm 64:8 Living Insights Bible

Who is the "he" the Psalter refers to? The part of us that cannot lie, that refuses to lie, that knows only the light.

> He whose tongue is deceitful falls into trouble.
> —Proverbs 21:23 Living Insights Bible

Chapter Seven

Different Ways the Ramseys Bury Themselves—a Cross Reference Guide (AKA the Smoking Guns)

This section serves as a cross-reference or guide. For example, there are twenty-six "smoking guns"—evidence that includes the Ramsey's involvement in JonBenet's murder; their involvement in planning the ransom note; the father's statements of sexually using JonBenet; the mother's admission of **seen that rape**. The Ramseys' unconscious statements of their efforts to cover up the crime also are part of this section. Many times the Ramseys talk about the murder of JonBenet (this is a double-category found under SMOKING GUN and CONFESSION). They speak about their efforts to fool the police investigators; Jon and Patsy make public statements to deceive the public, with the intention of winning the public to their side. Like O.J. Simpson, the Ramseys repeatedly state they are looking for the killers of their daughter by hiring an investigative team. The psychological states of mind are found in this section.

Some of the parents' forward statements contain multiple reversals that fit into different categories. For example, the forward statement by Jon Ramsey says, "It comes from knowing that the only way my family can move on now is to resolve why, who, how this happened." The reversals fit into four categories. They are the father's perception of himself—**you're a bad person**; marital discord—**was there no winner?** Sexual molestation—**molest** and Jon's perception of his wife—**her slavery**.

This section follows the same format regarding reversals as the previous ones. All of the Ramsey's forward comments are in quotation marks while the reversals follow the protocol by appearing in **bold type**.

Anxiety. Jon, forward, "we received cards from Canada, Europe, certainly all of the United States. I have corresponded several times with a little girl."
His reversal, **I scared.**

The father has plenty to be scared about. See Chapters Three and Five for the detailed analysis.

Patsy, forward, on the British documentary, "I hadn't heard any of that and like I say I was in really bad shape."

Patsy's reversal. **...and this is the riot and here it comes.** She's worried about being discovered.

Anxiety. Also see Smoking gun fifteen (listed alphabetically).

Confession. Patsy, forward, "We feel that there are at least two people on the face of the earth that know who did this and that is the killer and someone else that person may have confided in."

Patsy's reversal, **Oh I'm that person.**
The other two reversals are analyzed in Chapter Three, "The Ramseys Fatal Flaw."
Jon, forward, "At least up until yesterday any time spent looking at us is time wasted and that in part is why we brought in an investigative team as well to immediately look in other directions."
Jon's reversal, **Oh I done it.**
His second reversal involves a lie and is cross-referenced under LYING. An analysis of both reversals in found in Chapter Three: "The Ramseys Fatal Flaw."

Patsy, forward, "America has just been hurt so deeply with this."

Her revealing reversal, **our crime.**

Jon, forward, "to those of you who may want to ask, let me address you very directly. I did not kill my daughter, JonBenet."

Jon's reversal, **Serve evil.**

Patsy, forward, "I'm Patsy Ramsey, JonBenet's mother."

Patsy's reversal, **And I planned the note.**

Patsy, forward "the ad that we place in our local paper this weekend. This reward money has been offered since the death of JonBenet, but we feel like it wasn't got out to the public enough, so this ad with her most recent kindergarten picture will be featuring more frequently."

Patty's reversal, **I know you've sinned.**

Jon, forward, "I want whatever resources I can bring to bare, brought to bare."

Two reversals, one a confession, **That little crime messed up**; the other a lie, **Kill the source.** Both are analyzed in Chapter Three, "The Ramseys Fatal Flaw."

Jon, forward, "we think we're a normal American family that loves and values their children."

Two reversals, **Your life, a crime.** The second reversal, **hormone,** is cross-referenced under SEX ABUSE.

Jon, forward, "I opened the door and I turned the light on. I hoped that she was still OK but I could tell she wasn't."

Four reversals. Molest has a confessional ring to it. The other three are analyzed in Chapters Three and Five. They are also cross-referenced in this section —Was there no winner. Her slavery. You're a bad person.

Jon, forward, "...we want to thank those people that care about us..."

Reversal, **our rape hurt.**

Patsy, forward, "We were just frantic and I immediately—I dialed the police 911."

Reversal, **you sealed the bad here.** She's referring to hiding JonBenet's body in a remote room of the basement. (See Chapters Three and Five).

The second reversal in Patsy's comment was **you lady mannequin.** This is cross-referenced under VIEWPOINT, MOTHER. See Chapter Three for a detailed analysis of **you lady mannequin.**

Patsy, forward, "I was out of my mind and it said don't call the police, that type of thing."

Patsy's reversal, **Sealed the lock.** This is similar and consistent with her previous use of the word **seal** when she said, through her unconscious **you sealed the bad here.**

The interviewer to Jon Ramsey on the British documentary, "Did you have anything to do with the death of JonBenet?"

Jon Ramsey's answer, "No, we did not."

Jon Ramsey's reversal. **And I'd be the one.**

Patsy, on the British documentary where she's talking about the ransom note, "It's just kind of wasn't registering that somewhere it said we have your daughter."

Patsy's reversal. **This bitch did it** (wrote the confession note).

Jon Ramsey, forward, on the British documentary, discussing his reason for obtaining legal counsel. "What in the world for?"

Jon Ramsey's reversal. **Yes, and I am the one.**

Conning and Fooling. Jon, forward, "at least up until yesterday anytime spent looking at us is time wasted and that in part is why we brought in an investigative team to immediately look in other directions."

Two lies in the reversal. **I done it. It's a show you're running.** (Note. **I done it** also is cross-referenced under **Lying**).

Patsy, forward, "We feel that there are at least two people on the face of the earth that know who did this and that is the killer and someone else that person may have confided in."

This contains three reversals. **Oh I'm that person. Safe and I'll beat this. Seen that rape.** Her effort to fool and con the public is the reversal **Oh I'm that person.** This is also cross-referenced under LYING. **Safe and**

I'll beat this is cross-referenced under SELF-DECEPTION while RAPE is under SEX and CONFESSION.

Oh I'm that person. Stated another way, Patsy Ramsey is one of the two people that knows who committed the crime. In the second reversal Patsy says, **Safe and I'll beat this.** As we proceed with the Chapter Eight, "Closing Arguments," Patsy claims again and again that she does not feel **safe**; that she does not feel she will **beat this**.

The third revealing reversal states, **Seen that rape.** She is unable to clear her mind of the recurring images of JonBenet being betrayed by the girl's father and Patsy's husband. The disturbing pictures in her mind refuse to go away.

Patsy, forward, "I called our closest friends and they didn't even ask, I said come."

Her reversal, **This is a plan. Defended it.**

Other examples of the Ramseys conning and fooling the public are found in reversals like **and I planned the note** (Patsy, referring to the ransom note); **sounding the lie loose** (Jon, referring to his correspondence with a little girl); **got to sell you** (Jon, referring to his denial that he sexually molested his daughter); **they love it** (Jon, referring to his contempt for the police).

Another example of CONNING and FOOLING the public and media is found in Patsy's song contains the forward words and discloses the four revealing reversals. See Chapter Three. This is also cross-referenced under IRONY.

Drugs. Mom's forward statement. "It was difficult but they need to know, our handprints are all over our home."

Patsy's two related reversals, **Like my drugs. I rely on this.**

She turned to drugs to ease the difficult situation created from JonBenet's death. She relies on drugs, the second reversal, supports the first one. "Our handprints" is another reference to the drugs being all over the house, creating easy availability. Fantasy. Jon, forward, "…it's just been wonderful, so we've come out of this perhaps differently than you would expect in believing that there really is a lot of goodness in the world. And that's been an outcome that I think we certainly wouldn't have anticipated with this kind of tragedy."

Four reversals are uncovered here. **Nice little girl. Let me look. Let me nurse you. You get down on my fire.**

The father's sexual fantasy is about a young girl who has been corresponding him since JonBenet's death. The detailed analysis is found in Chapter Three. Also see under the Sex listing.

Fear. Jon, forward, "…at least up until yesterday anytime spent looking at us is time wasted and that in part is why we brought in an investigative team as well to immediately look in other directions."

Four reversals in this statement. One of them reflects fear, **I was the drop man.** He's afraid that his wife will gain the sympathy of the jury if they are prosecuted in a criminal trial. He knows the public is responding warmly to his wife and coldly to him. He believes he will be convicted with the maximum sentence—death. "The Ramseys Fatal Flaw" contains a detailed analysis of his "secret" fears. Jon, forward, "we received cards from Canada, Europe, certainly all of the United States…"

Two related reversals, **I scared, sounding the lie loose.** The first meaning is apparent. **…lie loose**, his lies and attempts to cover up the crime will prove futile. His lies will come back to haunt him.

Jon, forward, "…we know that there's many people that are praying for us…"

One of the reversals reflects his fear, **Must they warn me.**

Grief. See Suffering.

Guilt. Jon, forward, "I opened the door and I turned the light on. I hoped that she was still OK but I could tell she wasn't."

Jon Ramsey's reversal, **You're a bad person.**

Irony. Jon Ramsey forward, I want whatever resources I can bring to bare, brought to bare…"

Two reversals, one of them is a smoking gun number eleven. **Kill the source. That little crime messed up.**

The resources he intends to bring to the investigation are designed to serve as a smoke screen. Like O.J., he wants to show the American people his commitment to bring the killer to justice. The irony and double meaning of this message, **kill the source**, is that he, Jon Ramsey, is the source. He is killing himself. This will be discussed in Chapter Eight, "Closing Arguments."

Patsy sings the song that contains four damning reversals. One of the reversals includes the word **dammit.** When the same word is found forward and backward, Reverse Speech sees this as a evidence of a double indictment. (See Chapter Three, "The Ramseys Fatal Flaw" for the in-depth analysis of the four reversals found in the song.)

One of the ironic twists comes from Patsy singing an upbeat ditty in her forward voice while in her mind she dwells on her misery. Forward, she wants people to think that she is a happy person.

Jon, forward, "We'll find you (talking to the public during the CNN interview). We will find you. I have that as a sole mission for the rest of my life."

His reversal, **We now fool you.** On one level, he is happy with himself for fooling the public. On another level, his psyche is communicating—but Jon is not listening—that he is **fool**ing himself. This is reminiscent of William Blake's ironic observation that "a fool who persists in his folly will become wise."

Lying. Jon, forward, "I want whatever resources I can bring to bare, brought to bare."

Reversal, **Kill the source.**

Jon, "At least up until yesterday any time spent looking at us is time wasted and that in part is why we brought in an investigative team as well to immediately look in other directions."

Jon, reversal, **It's a show you're running**.

Jon, forward, "There have been innuendoes that she has been or was sexually molested. I can tell you they were the most hurtful innuendoes to us as a family."

Reversal, **know for the next time but they're so ugly yes**. The next time he becomes involved with a minor he will be careful.

Jon, forward, "...we received cards from Canada, Europe, certainly all of the United States. I have corresponded several times with a little girl..."

Two reversals here. **I scared, sounding the lie loose. I scared** is cross-referenced under SCARED.

Jon, forward, "...I want whatever resources I can bring to bare, brought to bare."

His reversal, **kill the source**. He doesn't want to truth out. **Kill the source** (the truth).

Jon, forward, "...to those of you who may want to ask, let me address you very directly. I did not kill my daughter, JonBenet..." One of his reversals says, **Got to sell you**. The press conference is designed to fool the public.

Jon, forward, "...this was a process that the police went through with us as suspects. I don't believe any new information was provided that we hadn't provided very early on."

Two revealing reversals, **They love it. Silly sham**. The first reflects his arrogant attitude toward the police. The second is another example of staging the conference to deceive the public.

Jon, forward, "...then I went downstairs and discovered her body."

The reversal. **I've answered none of your points**.

Marital Discord. The following "marital discord" reversal was found in the Category Confession.

The reversal is **her slavery**.

It becomes tiresome for a perpetual winner, the master (Jon Ramsey) to experience the same predictable situation from his slave (Patsy Ramsey), making both of them a loser in their unholy alliance.

Not Lying. Jon, forward, "One of the detectives asked me and my friend who was there to go through every inch of the house asking us to do that more to give us something to do. Started in the basement and we're just looking and, we had one room in the basement."

Two reversals here. **Search with them. Then he calls his unit.** In his mind, Jon is re-living the crime.

Jon is to be congratulated for delivering forty-nine words where he tells the whole truth and nothing but the truth. However, his psyche continues to push him toward the light, as will be seen in Chapter Eight, "Closing Arguments."

Jon did not lie in his above reversals. Neither is his wife. Patsy, forward, "we have just basically read or watched very little. You can't. It's just overwhelming, we're grieving, and it's hurtful. I can't tell you how bad it is."

Two more reversals here, **Cut up spirit. Spirit wolf bursting.** She is speaking the truth in her forward comments. As mentioned in the analysis section in Chapter Three, her daytime memories reflect the intensity of her dreams and nightmares over her involvement in JonBenet's death. A psychiatric ambulance needs to be summoned. Day and night, her flesh, spirit and emotions are involved in the mother's pain.

Pain. See Suffering.

Rape. See Sex.

Scared. See Anxiety.

Self-Deception. Patty, forward, "We feel that there are at least two people on the face of the earth that know who did this and that is the killer and someone else that person may have confided in."

The reversal shows she is deceiving herself, **Safe and I'll beat this.** There are four reversals here. (See CONNING).

Sex. Jon, forward, "…we think we're a normal American family that loves and values their children."

Reversal, **hormone.** This is analyzed in Part Three.

Jon, forward, "I opened the door and I turned the light on. I hoped that she was still OK but I could tell she wasn't."

Reversal, **Molest** indicates that he hopes that no sign of sexual wrongdoing will be uncovered when the child's body is located.

Jon, forward, "it's just been wonderful, so we've come out of this perhaps differently than you would expect in believing that there really is a lot of goodness in the world. And that's been an outcome that I think we certainly wouldn't have anticipated with this kind of tragedy."

Four devastating reversals by Jon Ramsey, **Nice little girl. Let me look. Let me nurse you. You get down on my fire.** See "The Ramseys Fatal Flaw" for a detailed analysis.

Sex. Also see Viewpoint (JonBenet is her dad's sex slave).

Jon, forward, "There have been innuendoes that she has been or was sexually molested. I can tell you they were the most hurtful innuendoes to us as a family."

One of the reversals, **know for the next time,** indicates he will be careful to avoid detection on his next sexual foray. Cross-reference SEX, UNCONTROLLED.

Sexual Desire. Patsy, forward, "We feel that there are at least two people on the face of the earth..."

One of the three reversals focuses on the sexual abuse of JonBenet, **Seen that rape.**

Patsy, forward, "America has just been hurt so deeply with this."

Her reversal, **our crime.** See cross-references **Confession** and **Smoking Gun.**

Our crime may also refer to Patsy's knowledge and approval of her husband using JonBenet as his sex toy.

Sex, Uncontrolled. This is a separate category that belongs exclusively to Jon Ramsey. His forward statement, "to those of you who may want to ask, let me address very directly, I did not kill my daughter, JonBenet. There have also been innuendoes that she has been or was sexually molested. I can tell you they were the most hurtful to us as a family."

There are four revealing reversals here. **Nice little girl. Let me look. Let me nurse you. You get down on my fire.** (See Chapter Three for a detailed analysis.)

Smoking gun one. Patsy, forward, "We feel that there are at least two people on the face of the earth that know who did this and that is the killer and someone else that person may have confided in."

Her reversal, **Oh I'm that person.**

Smoking gun two. Jon, forward, "...at least up until yesterday anytime spent looking at us is time wasted and that in part is why we brought in an investigative team as well to immediately look in other directions."

His reversal, **I done it.**

Smoking guns three and four. Jon, forward, "I opened the door and turned the light on. I hoped that she was OK but I could tell she wasn't."

His reversals, **Molest. You're a bad person.**

Smoking gun five. Jon forward, "I want whatever resources I can bring to bare, brought to bare."

His reversal, **That little crime messed up.**

Smoking gun six. Patsy, forward, "America has just been hurt so deeply with this."

Her reversal, **our crime.**

Smoking gun seven. Jon, forward, "…we think we're a normal American family that loves and values their children …"

His reversal, **your life, a crime.**

Smoking gun eight. Patsy, forward, "…we have just basically read or watched very little. You can't. It's just overwhelming, we're grieving, and it's hurtful. I can't tell you how bad it is."

Her reversal, **I did it.**

Smoking gun nine. Patsy, forward, "We feel that there are at least two people on the face of the earth…"

Her reversal, **Seen that rape.** This indicates her knowledge of JonBenet's sexual assault by her husband.

Smoking gun ten. Jon, forward, "…we want to thank those people that care about us…"

His reversal, **our rape hurt.**

Smoking gun eleven. Patsy, forward, "…but let me assure you that I did not kill JonBenet. I did not have anything to do with it…"
Her reversal, **your shame. You feel it.**

Smoking gun twelve. Patsy, forward, "I'm Patsy Ramsey, JonBenet's mother…"
Her reversal, **And I planned the note.**

Smoking gun thirteen. Patsy, forward, "…the ad that we placed in our local paper this weekend. This reward money…"
Her reversal, **I know you've sinned.**

Smoking gun fourteen. Patsy, forward, "America has just been hurt so deeply with this."
The revealing reversal, **Our crime.**

Smoking gun fifteen. Jon, forward, "The American public has been led to believe that while we went to bed that night before Christmas, brutally beat JonBenet, sexually molested her, strangled her, then went to sleep, got up the next morning, wrote a three-page ransom note…

Smoking gun sixteen. Jon's reversal. **That night was hell. We wound the deal/you'll want the garbage.** He is telling us that the American public has been led to believe that while we went to bed and that someone entered the house and killed JonBenet.

Smoking gun seventeen. The interviewer to Jon: "Did you have anything to do with the death of JonBenet?"
Jon Ramsey, "No, we did not."
His reversal. **And I'd be the one.**

Smoking gun eighteen. …I had the note This is Jon's reversal where he is talking to the interviewer in the British documentary that is discussed in Chapter Five. The ransom note is one of six reversals that were found in Jon's forward statement.

Smoking gun nineteen. Patsy is talking in the British documentary. "It's just kind of wasn't registering that somewhere it said we have your daughter" (the ransom note says the kidnappers have JonBenet).

One of the reversals she refers to the ransom note—**this bitch did it.**

Smoking gun twenty. In the British documentary Patsy tells the interviewer that she and her husband are wondering what to do. She is referring to the ransom note that stated they are not to involve the police. The note said "if you even talk to a stray dog, she dies."

Her reversal. **I had need to swab the seal, maybe. Swab**—to hide the evidence before contacting the police. **Seal**—to protect themselves from being found out.

Smoking gun twenty-one. A second reversal was found in the "smoking gun twenty" discussed above. The second reversal was **swab**—to hide the evidence before contacting the police.

Smoking gun twenty-two. Jon Ramsey is talking to the interviewer in the British documentary. The subject focuses on obtaining legal counsel. "What in the world for?" Jon said to the interviewer.

Jon Ramsey's reversal. **Yes, and I am the one.** The reversal indicates that Jon knew he needed counsel because he was guilty.

Jon immediately follows this with, "We began to realize we are suspects. I was okay with that because I assumed it was a broad investigation."

The interviewer said to Jon, "So you have by this time begun to conclude that people were beginning to point the finger at you."

Jon, "We were hearing that from our friends.

Jon's reversal. **I'm hearing through you.** He's acknowledging that his friends are doubtful of his innocence.

Patsy, "I hadn't heard any of that and like I say I was in really bad shape."

On the TV she is emotional, waving her husband to keep quiet. She realizes he blew it by what he said. In her mind Patsy sees the deluge coming.

Patsy's reversal. **Yes, I be heard and this is the riot and here it comes.**

She states that one of her friend's said that people are talking about her and Jon being involved in JonBenet's death. Her friend doesn't want Patsy to be upset.

Smoking gun twenty-three. In the British documentary Patsy is telling the interviewer about a comment made by one of his friends. "I'm going to tell you this and I don't want you to get upset. But they're saying and it's being reported that you and Jon may have been involved in JonBenet's death."

Patsy's reversal. **Oh I done it.**

Smoking gun twenty-four. The British documentary cuts to Patsy talking about the day at the supermarket when her son saw the tabloid article that accused the parents of murdering JonBenet.

Patsy, "He (her son Burke) was blank and he just sort of looked away…"

Patsy's reversal. **It's no accident.** She confesses that the killing was planned.

Smoking gun twenty-five. The British interviewer asked Patsy to comment on the report in the tabloids that the parents because of a bedwetting problem killed JonBenet.

Patsy, "It is so minuscule compared to me going through advanced ovarian cancer."

She emphasizes "so."

Patsy's reversal. **Oh, us did it.**

Smoking gun twenty-six. See the Afterword **I caused the head wound.**

Suffering. Patsy, forward, "…but let me assure you that I did not have anything to do with it…"

Two reversals here, both reflect suffering, **Your shame. You feel it.**

Patsy, forward, "I'd like to take a moment to just let you know how much we have appreciated the hundreds and hundreds of cards and letters and pictures that children have sent me, little angels and books, that wonderfully compassionate caring people from all over the world has sent to us."

Patsy, two reversals. **Dad's myth was our promise. Soul wished mess.** In these reversals, this technology is speaking through the language of the soul and reflect nightmare messages. The intensity, duration and frequency of this emotion reaches melancholia. The detailed analysis of these seeming innocuous reversals are found in Chapter Three.

Patsy, forward, "…quite frankly, over the past months it has not been real easy to talk with anyone…"

Patsy, two reversals. **I'm still a snob. I don't mean it.** Once again, intense psychological and spiritual suffering are expressed. Like the previous reversals, **Dad's myth was our promise. Soul wished mess,** review the hidden meaning in Chapter Three.

Patsy, forward, "we have just basically read or watched very little. You can't. It's just overwhelming, we're grieving, and it's hurtful. I can't tell you how bad it is."

Patsy, two reversals. **Cut up spirit. Spirit wolf bursting.** She is speaking the truth in her forward comments. As mentioned in the analysis section in Chapter Three, her daytime memories reflect the intensity of her dreams and nightmares over her involvement in JonBenet's death. A psychiatric ambulance needs to be summoned. Day and night, her flesh, spirit and emotions are involved in the mother's pain.

Patsy, forward, "There is a killer on the loose…keep your babies close to you."

Her reversal, **Feel the knot.** the knot in her stomach.

Patsy, forward, "It was difficult but they need to know, our handprints are all over our home."

Her reversals, **Like my drugs. I rely on this.**

To numb her from the relentless suffering, drugs are all over the house, making them easily accessible.

Patsy, in her song that with the upbeat ditty.

> You say neither
> I say neither
> Either, either
> Neither, neither
> Let's call the whole thing off

Patsy has six reversals in the ditty. **wrong at the heart. Fast and under and evil number and each carry on yet dammit, try feeding ya.** Contrast her forward and reversals by referring to the analysis in Chapter Three.

Jon, forward, "I opened the door and I turned the light on. I hoped that she was still OK but I could tell she wasn't."

Four reversals are found here. **Was there no winner. Her slavery. Molest. You're a bad person.**

Molest indicates that he hopes that no sign of sexual wrongdoing will be uncovered when the child's body is located. **You're a bad person** suggests Jon's suffering. Or does it indicate his recognition that he may be discovered as the perpetuator of the crimes against JonBenet? This is discussed further in "Closing Arguments," along with the number of references to suffering made by the husband and wife.

The Truth. See Not Lying.

Sexual Molestation. See Sex.

Viewpoint. Jon, forward, "I opened the door and I turned the light on. I hoped that she was still OK but I could tell she wasn't.

Reversal, **her slavery.** JonBenet was his sex slave.

Viewpoint, Patsy. "We were just frantic and I immediately, I dialed the police, 911.

Reversal, **you lady mannequin.** This is ripe with meaning. See "What is Reverse Speech and Embedded Communication" and Chapter Three for a detailed analysis.

Chapter Eight

Closing Arguments[1]

Lie Detector Vs. Reverse Speech

Reverse Speech is connected with the psyche and analyzes the speech of the person. The lie detector measures the physiological response of the person being studied.

The lie detector occasionally can be controlled and manipulated by the conscious mind while the Reverse Speech technology is beyond the control and manipulation of the conscious mind. Refer to the experiments that were performed, where attempts were made to deliberately lie to the psyche. The experiments were broadcast over the radio show produced and hosted by Richard Rubacher and Gail Wilts. The information is found in Chapter Four: "Highlights of Our Weekly Radio Show."

By incorporating the evidence produced by the conscious and unconscious in these Closing Arguments, we enter a broader perspective that takes into account spiritual reality as well as material reality. The totality of the person is presented, which includes the dark side of the self, the collective unconscious and the personal unconscious.

Through Reverse Speech technology, we become witnesses to the communication exchange that takes place between the ego and the unconscious.

---

1. The reader is the spiritual judge. You are presented with the arguments in the Spiritual Court that tries the Ramseys.

As we proceed to the climax of these Closing Arguments, we will see there is within us a Force greater than the will of our ego that constitutes ten percent of our consciousness.

The Spiritual Outlaw

In our weekly radio program, *Dance With Your Shadow*, we feature a segment called "The Spiritual Court of Law." Through Reverse Speech, the radio audience hears the hidden motives and secret agenda of the person who is on trial. One of the hosts of the show, Richard Rubacher or Gail Wilts, pounds the gavel and announces, "Hear Ye, Hear Ye, Hear Ye, the Spiritual Court of Law is now in session."

The defendant takes his place in the imaginary courtroom. We then ask for the spiritual judges (the radio audience) to take their place next to the radio.

The spiritual judges in the radio studio, Rubacher and Wilts, in a soft voice, ask for silence while the Spiritual Court is in session. We urge drivers to pull their cars over, as heavy-duty concentration is required.

We remind the radio audience, now known as the spiritual judges, that in the traditional court of law, attorneys for both sides probe the conscious mind. This aspect of the mind, referred to as the tip of the iceberg, has severe limitations. Exploration of the conscious, rational mind cannot access the hidden agenda and secret motives that are buried in the unconscious. Nor will the hidden agenda and dark motives be honestly presented in a forthright manner by the defendant or other witnesses. As we know, people lie to protect themselves or to prevent harm from coming to someone they care about. Another difficulty in dealing with the conscious mind is that a person may forget an event. Even motives are elusive due to defense mechanisms of repression and suppression. We realize that a person may not be consciously aware of why he or she acted in a certain way. Things like shame, fear of exposure, humiliation and other factors are detected in the Spiritual Court.

Through this technology that eavesdrops on the psyche, the vastness of the *submerged iceberg known as the unconscious* becomes open to public scrutiny. We are able to place the defendants on the "witness stand." Their physical presence is not essential. Their "vibrational signature" is in attendance—through the tape recorded statements the totality of the consciousness of Jon and Patsy Ramsey are measured, analyzed and available for public exposure. Their persona (their mask) is stripped away, as are their defense mechanisms.

We do not require the defendants to take an oath that they will tell the truth, the whole truth and nothing but the truth. By peering into the psyche, access to the vastness of their being is available. The penetrating exploration of the unconscious enables us to access the nightmares and scary dreams of the Ramseys. By probing into the previously inaccessible regions of the parents' psyche, we are provided with information about the recurring thoughts that haunt the Ramseys. The disturbing thoughts that suddenly appear on the screen of their conscious minds during their waking hours are also made available to us.

Through this technology, the private thoughts of the Ramseys are no longer private. The "secret" feelings, desires and fantasies of the parents are also made public.

The parents can hide their true thoughts and feelings in a traditional court of law. Not so in the Spiritual Court of Law.

While the conscious mind is the tip of the iceberg and makes up ten percent of the personality, we recognize that this ten percent is to be analyzed and held sacred. Thus we honor the Ramseys by making multiple references to the testimony given in their forward remarks (home of the conscious mind).

Hear Ye! Hear Ye! The Spiritual Court of Law is now in session.

At the outset we would like to congratulate Jon Ramsey when he made the following statement: Jon, forward, "One of the detectives asked me and my friend who was there to go through every inch of the house asking us to do that more to give us something to do. Started in the basement and we're just looking and, we had one room in the basement."

As discussed previously (Chapter Three: "The Ramseys Fatal Flaw"), two messages are uncovered from the unconscious of Jon Ramsey's quoted statement. His psyche states: **Search with them. Then he calls his unit.**

Jon is re-living the scene as he escorts the police. After the unsuccessful search, the police contact headquarters in Boulder, Colorado.

This is a rare event. Jon Ramsey is telling the truth. His conscious mind (the ego) and his unconscious (the psyche) are in harmony.

These forty-nine words demonstrate that the defendant, Jon Ramsey, is psychologically intact. He is of sound mind.

These forty-nine words expressed by his conscious ego are not contradicted by his unconscious. This indicates that Jon Ramsey's feelings *as an evolved human being are undeveloped.* His feeling nature, which demonstrates an open heart, and his emotional outlook on life are that of a child. He displays no remorse. There is no sense of shame.

What is true of Jon Ramsey is not true of his wife. Her feeling nature is adequately developed. That is why she resorted to drugs (please refer to Chapter Seven, under "Drugs" for detailed information why she resorted to drugs to ease the pain and bury the memories of her actions toward JonBenet). She tried to numb herself from the pain of what she did. Her sense of shame haunts her.

With these preliminary points made, it is time to proceed.

If the Ramseys are innocent of any wrongdoing in the death of their daughter, why would Patsy Ramsey make the statement **I did it?**

We ask you to review the evidence given where Patsy says in her forward voice, "…we have just basically read or watched very little. You can't. It's just overwhelming, we're grieving, and it's hurtful. I can't tell you how bad it is."

Her forward statement is honest, direct, simple and cuts to the essence of her suffering. The pain is genuine.

A probe into the psyche fails to support the statement made by her conscious mind. We find two messages from the psyche. **Yes, I did it. Spirit wolf bursting.**

The first reversal **Yes, I did it** is clear and distinct. *Smoking gun number one* is expressed with such conviction that it will send her to the gallows.

Once again, in Patsy's forward statement, she tells us "…It's just overwhelming, we're grieving, and it's hurtful. I can't tell you how bad it is." What she is unable to express in her forward voice explodes to the surface with the depths of her psyche. We understand the reason for her profound grief and suffering that torments her.

The message from the psyche is telegraphic It contains three words. **Spirit wolf bursting.**

Spirit refers to the totality of our being, the male and female aspects of our mind, where the male is the symbol of the intellect and female is the symbol of our intuitive self. This is another reference to the analogy Abraham Lincoln used about the house divided against itself cannot stand. (See Patsy's forward statement and the reversal. Her forward says, "the police and investigators have assured us that this is a case which can be solved. You may be eluding the authorities for a time but God knows who you are and we will find you.")

Cut off from her **spirit**, she is exiled in the wilderness, isolated in a barren country, starving in a spiritual wasteland.

When the two revealing reversals are considered together, the intensity, duration and frequency of her suffering is staggering. Patsy Ramsey's heart is shredded, torn apart. While the heart continues to function on a physical level, the force behind the heart does not beat. Without a **spirit**, life is empty of joy.

In this technology, when **wolf** appears in a reversal, an alarm sounds, signaling very deep spiritual concerns, which can be healthy or disastrous, depending on the context. This is a powerful phrase of the psyche. When **spirit wolf bursting** appears in a reversal, a person is without any psychological armor or spiritual protection. To a Reverse Speech Analyst, this is viewed as a 911 emergency. The psyche is telling the conscious mind or ego that his or her life has no direction. The motivation for living is gone. Patsy Ramsey requires immediate psychiatric help and spiritual counseling.

Suffering intensified

Would Patsy Ramsey admit to her suffering if she was not involved in the killing of her daughter? In Chapter Seven, "Different Ways the Ramseys Bury Themselves," under the category of 'Suffering,' her reversals betray her forward comments time after time. In her forward voice she says, "…but let me assure you that I did not have anything to do with it (the murder)…"

Her psyche—the part of her that is divine, that never lies tells a different story. **Your shame, you feel it.**

When Patsy said in her forward remark, "There is a killer on the loose," her unconscious betrays her with the revealing reversal, **Feel the knot.** This is the knot in her stomach. This is her physiological reaction to her emotional state.

Jon Ramsey does not appear once in the 'Suffering section' of Chapter Seven, "Different Ways the Ramseys Bury Themselves." He is pre-occupied with concerns like being caught for telling repeated lies about his involvement in the killing of JonBenet. **I scared.** He is pre-occupied with the cover-up of the evidence at the crime scene. **That little crime messed up.** In his mind he goes over his sexual activity with his daughter. **Serve evil. Our rape hurt. Molest.**

The smoking guns

Members of the spiritual jury, do you remember how many smoking guns the divine self of Jon and Patsy Ramsey have surfaced? The number is twenty-six. Here they are some of them, extracted from Chapters Three and Five.

Smoking gun number 1, Patsy, forward, "We feel that there are at least two people on the face of the earth that know who did this and that is the killer and someone else that person may have confided in."

Her divine says, **Oh I'm that person.** Smoking gun number 2. Jon, forward, "...at least up until yesterday anytime spent looking at us is time wasted and that in part is why we brought in an investigative team as well to immediately look in other directions."

His divine self speaks, **I done it.**

Smoking gun numbers 3 and 4. Jon, forward, "I opened the door and turned the light on. I hoped that she was OK but I could tell she wasn't."

His divine self, **Molest. You're a bad person.**

Smoking gun number 5. Jon forward, "I want whatever resources I can bring to bare, brought to bare."

His divine self, **That little crime messed up.**

Smoking gun number 6. Patsy, forward, "America has just been hurt so deeply with this."

Her divine self, **our crime.**

Smoking gun number 7. Jon, forward, "...we think we're a normal American family that loves and values their children ..."

His divine self, **your life, a crime.**

Smoking gun number 8. Patsy, "...we have just basically read or watched very little. You can't. It's just overwhelming, we're grieving, and it's hurtful. I can't tell you how bad it is."

Her divine self, **I did it.**

Smoking gun number 9. Patsy, forward, "We feel that there are at least two people on the face of the earth..."

Her divine self, **Seen that rape.** This indicates her knowledge of JonBenet's sexual assault by her husband.

Smoking gun number 10. Jon, "...we want to thank those people that care about us..."

His divine self, **our rape hurt.**

Smoking gun number 11. Patsy, forward, "...but let me assure you that I did not kill JonBenet. I did not have anything to do with it..."

Her divine self, **your shame. You feel it.**

Smoking gun number 12. Patsy, "I'm Patsy Ramsey, JonBenet's mother..."

Her divine self, **And I planned the note.**

Smoking gun number 13. Patsy, "...the ad that we placed in our local paper this weekend. This reward money..."

Her divine self, **I know you've sinned.**

You, members of the spiritual jury, can refer to the other thirteen smoking guns that are found in Chapter Seven.

A review of the Ramseys' words

If Jon Ramsey had nothing to do with murdering his daughter why would the divine aspect of his being shout **I done it**? Why would the next statement in the same reversal contain these words—**It's a show you're running**?

Members of the spiritual jury, we will "re-play" more of the self-incriminating evidence presented by the two defendants. Jon Ramsey, "at least up until yesterday anytime spent looking at us is time wasted and that in part is why we brought in an investigative team as well to immediately look in other directions."

His divine self speaks, **I done it. It's a show you're running.**

If Patsy Ramsey has no knowledge of JonBenet's death, why would there be such an inconsistency between what she said in her forward voice and the damning testimony provided in her reversal?

Members of the spiritual jury, we will "re-play" Patsy's statement, "We feel that there are at least two people on the face of the earth that know who did this and that is the killer and someone else that person may have confided in."

Her divine voice speaks, **Oh I'm that person. Safe and I'll beat this. Seen that rape.**

Oh I'm that person. Stated another way, Patsy Ramsey is one of at two people that knows who committed the crime. In the second message from her divinity, we have, **Safe and I'll beat this.** As we proceed with the Closing Arguments, we will hear her say again and again that she does not feel **safe**; that she does not feel she will **beat this.**

The third revealing reversal in her statement, **Seen that rape.** She is unable to clear her mind of the recurring images of JonBenet being betrayed by the girl's father and Patsy's husband. The disturbing pictures in her mind refuse to go away.

Here is Jon Ramsey, "...to those of you who may want to ask let me address very directly. I did not kill my daughter, JonBenet."

Now let us tune in to "the words behind the words" that T.S. Eliot described in his 1920 poem, *Gerontion*. His divine self coughs up four messages. **And the mikes are all dumb. Voice found it out. Serve evil. Now we hate.**

Mikes are all dumb refers to the media (**mikes**) as being the dumb ones, since he appears to be having his way. The press representatives have not interrupted him with challenging questions.

Jon Ramsey's next admission tantalizes us. While he is confident about orchestrating the media, his unconscious torments him. Doubt now engulfs him. **Voice found it out** indicates that breaking the silence may have catastrophic results for him and Patsy.

Like a nightmare or scary dream, Reverse Speech is dreadful and wonderful. When we fail to "get the message" the nightmare is giving us, there is dread and panic. When we do "get" the message, the nightmare or scary dream has become a wonderful friend. For example, falling in a lake and drowning is dreadful. The lake is a symbol for the emotional difficulty we refuse to face. By ignoring the problem, we are in effect drowning. By having the courage to face the difficulty, we will find the emotional strength to sail the troubled waters into a safe harbor.

The third message Jon Ramsey's divine self coughed up, **Serve evil**. His deception and deviousness are not truly helping him but are serving **evil**. This is another wake-up call to be truthful.

The fourth "hidden," **Now we hate**. This indicates there is venom in his and Patsy's heart. This is a result of fear of being caught.

"Your own mouth condemns you," Job 15:6. Jon Ramsey unconsciously is tying the knot around his neck.

JonBenet's deadly song re-visited

In American slang, "to sing" means blowing the whistle on someone. Through an ironic twist, JonBenet Ramsey sings a song that buries her parents. Hidden in the child's forward words is a tell tale message that opens the floodgates on the sexual crime committed against her.

We know about the message that the divine self of JonBenet shouted from the roof top, **Mommy, now I know evil love.**

Isn't it conceivable that **evil love** indicates JonBenet's grief over her parents' betrayal?

Isn't it also possible that the parents' unconscious minds picked up the message from their daughter's unconscious? Couldn't they have panicked in the veiled threat contained in the reversal? Isn't it also likely that the child's profound utterance **Mommy, now I know evil love** indicated that she intended to do something, like go public?

This is why Jon and Patsy Ramsey silenced her. But they did not succeed.

When the "psychological pulse" was taken to determine the American public's reaction to the Ramseys' appearances on the CNN press conferences, a bad feeling permeated the land. On television, the parents gave us their "persona." In Jungian terms, a persona—our mask or front—is how we wish to be seen by the world. It is our psychological clothing that hides our true self. An analogy is made with physical clothing we put on. Both are intended to convey an image to those we meet.

At the CNN press conferences, both of you presented your persona—the mask or front that you wear. That means we received the tip of the iceberg. By plunging to deeper levels, we learned what the divine spark within said. The sour taste is gone from our mouths. We no longer feel cheated.

Both of you will continue to have an opportunity to present your genuine and authentic Self in a future press conference. You can be "straight out" by telling us about your secret agenda and hidden motives.

By discarding your false self, your public personality, you will be on the road to becoming psychologically evolved and spiritually mature. Then the entire true story will be told and we will know what *really* happened and why.

There are many ways to achieve wholeness that results in healing. One method is to invite Reverse Speech or Embedded Communications analysts like the author and Gail Wilts into your home or jail cell. We will tape the communication exchange with your soul and play the reversals back to you. A remarkable event will occur as the inner voice talks to you in a way that provides comfort. We ask you to reflect on this opportunity to lose your life by healing your soul. "A house divided against itself cannot stand." A mind divided against itself cannot stand.

The New Testament tells us the alienation between the conscious and unconscious is a formula for disaster. "For he is our peace, who hath made both one, and hath broken down the middle wall or partition between us" (Ephesians 2:14). "He" is the Spirit that dwells within the sacred temple. "Made both one" is the conscious and unconscious or the male and female minds. When disconnected from the Source, a wall is built between the Spirit (God) and ourselves. This amounts to the creation of a Berlin Wall of the mind. Until that wall is bulldozed, neither of you will know about the "peace that passes understanding," which is what both of you yearn for in your reversals. The split of the psyche from the ego, your conscious and unconscious, is, in Biblical terms, creating hell on earth.

"What God has joined together, let no one take apart" (Matthew 19:6). When man, the conscious mind containing the ego and intellect, and woman, the unconscious mind, containing intuition and receptivity and the home of the dream center—when the conscious and unconscious are connected as one, peace and harmony reigns. The soul will no longer present disturbing nightmares and torturous thoughts complete with horrendous images to the conscious mind during during your waking hours. The drug you seek is found in the spirit that dwells within the holy temple. This higher authority is accessible to you in its awe-ful form through this technology.

Final thoughts on the dark side of the self

What is true of the dark side of the Ramseys has application to all of us. A psychological truth is exemplified—that what is denied or buried in the unconscious—returns as a dark power. The Ramseys deposited their dead daughter in the basement, which is symbolic of the unconscious. They shut the door, thinking their dark deed would remain hidden in the buried part of the psyche.

Not so. The denied thoughts and feelings dumped into the shadow "turn into devils and rattle the door and seek to find some way out of their imprisoned state and back into the world of consciousness."*

The writer of these words, Jon A. Sanford, continues his excellent observation:

> This attempt of repressed contents to reach consciousness is not simply an attempt to disturb consciousness or gain revenge.

---

* Jon A. Sanford, *Evil, The Shadow Side of Reality*. Crossroad Publishing, New York, NY, 1996, pp 124-125.

The movement is toward the light of consciousness because this is necessary if psychological redemption is to occur (my italics).

No matter how malignant these split-off contents of the psyche may appear to be, and no matter how malicious their tricks, there is always the possibility of redemption if they can reach consciousness.

Sanford concludes by stating the goal of the unconscious is to keep disturbing us until we get the message that we are to examine the darkness by holding it to the light. This way the dark side is integrated and the war of the conscious (male mind) and unconscious (female mind)—what we refer to as the "battle of the sexes"—comes to an end. The unaware ego is replaced by the aware ego. There is a psychological and spiritual triumph.

In conclusion, when we realize that we are more than we think we are, we will get on our knees and weep with wonder.

Bless God.

Bless the Ramseys—the mother, father, living son and JonBenet who is experiencing life after life.

Afterword

Afterword—speculation on the motive

The twenty-six "smoking guns" that appear in the book indicate Jon and Patsy Ramsey's involvement in the murder of JonBenet. We know about their cover up, lies and deception. The most damaging statement came from JonBenet's deadly song, "I want to be a cowboy singer." Her unconscious voice cried out, **...I know evil love.**

The second most damaging statement-which we failed to notice while analyzing the British documentary for an entire week-was brought to our attention three days after the manuscript was mailed to the publisher. We were able to include this unexpected finding in this section. An inner prompting led us to search the Reverse Speech website. Perhaps there was something we had overlooked during our two-year scrutiny of the Ramseys' public statements. We found it-the second most damaging statement-it came from Patsy. In the British documentary Patsy said, "We have had everything in our lives scoured. They have talked with my fourth-grade teacher."

Her reversal, **I caused the head wound.**

By making a public statement and allowing it to be tape recorded, she entered the confessional box, allowing her own voice to betray her.

How did she cause the head wound?

We speculate that Jon was engaged in a sexual act with JonBenet whenPatsy walked in on that fateful Christmas night in 1996. The father was putting JonBenet to bed. In the British interview Jon commented-in his forward speech-that he took his daughter to her room at bedtime. Following his usual ritual, "I prepared JonBenet for bed." In walked Patsy.

Seeing what was going on, she became enraged and threw something at Jon, accidentally hitting JonBenet in the head. The violence of the blow inflicted heavy damage to the little girl. The mishap also startled Jon and Patsy. Her revealing reversal, smoking gun twenty-six, **I caused the head wound**. The autopsy report notes that JonBenet's head was injured but the cause of death resulted from strangulation. We contend the death was not planned. Jon and Patsy panicked.

They conferred about seeking immediate medical attention by calling an ambulance or driving the injured child to the hospital. Questions about how the massive head injury occurred would have had to be answered. In their panic, the Ramseys literally "lost their heads" and proceeded to carry out the murder and then cover it up.

This is our version of what occurred at the time of JonBenet's death the molestation, the unexpected entrance of Patsy and her reaction of rage that set into motion the death of JonBenet on that fateful Christmas in 1996.

Appendix

Appendix A: "Reverse Speech...of Nobel Prize caliber"

LARRY DOSSEY, M.D.
6800 WOODMARK COURT
DALLAS, TEXAS 75230

October 19, 1989

TO WHOM IT MAY CONCERN:

I have recently become aware of the groundbreaking work of Mr. David Oates in the field of "reverse speech."

This is a form of communication lying completely outside conscious awareness. If it is validated — as I suspect it will be, after examining the evidence thus far — this discovery may prove to be of Nobel caliber.

It is rare that a truly novel, creative, and profoundly important discovery is made in the field of human communcation. These events are unusual, only a few in any century. Mr. Oates' stunning findings seem to fall into this category. While one's enthusiasm must be restrained as this idea is carefully elaborated and validated, it is difficult to not sense the excitement that is gathering around his unique work.

Larry Dossey, M.D.

Larry Dossey, M.D.

Diplomate, American Board of Internal Medicine

Author: *Recovering the Soul*
Beyond Illness
Space, Time and Medicine

Appendix B: The Ransom Note

Mr. Ramsey,

Listen carefully! We are a group of individuals that represent a small foreign faction. We respect your bussiness but not the country that it serves. At this time we have your daughter in our posession. She is safe and unharmed and if you want her to see 1997, you must follow our instructions to the letter.

You will withdraw $118,000.00 from your account. $100,000 will be in $100 bills and the remaining $18,000 in $20 bills. Make sure that you bring an adequate size attache to the bank. When you get home you will put the money in a brown paper bag. I will call you between 8 and 10 am tomorrow to instruct you on delivery. The delivery will be exhausting so I advise you to be rested. If we monitor you getting the money early, we might call you early to arrange an earlier delivery of the money and hence a earlier pick-up of your daughter. Any deviation of my instructions will result in the immediate execution of your daughter. You will also be denied her remains for proper burial. The two gentlemen watching over your daughter do not particularly like you so I advise you not to provoke them. Speaking to anyone about your situation, such as Police, F.B.I., etc., will result in your daughter being beheaded. If we catch you talking to a stray dog, she dies. If you alert bank authorities, she dies. If the money is in any way marked or tampered with, she dies. You will be scanned for electronic devices and if any are found, she dies. You can try to deceive us but be warned that we are familiar with law enforcement countermeasures and tactics. You stand a 99% chance of killing your daughter if you try to out smart us. Follow our instructions and you stand a 100% chance of getting her back. You and your family are under constant scrutiny as well as the authoriti Don't try to grow a brain John. You are not the only fat cat around so don't think that killing will be difficult. Don't underestimate us John. Use that good southern common sense of yours. It is up to you now John!

Victory!

S.B.T.C

Printed in the United Kingdom
by Lightning Source UK Ltd.
9621800001B